A
Spiritual Sex Manual

Given by God
to His Children
that They
Might find a better Way

A Spiritual Sex Manual

Published by
The Christ Foundation
P.O. Box 10
Port Angeles, Washington 98362
206/452-5249

3/97

Original Art: Rosemarie Fabina
Concept and Design: Reyna Moore & Associates
Typography and Layout: Qualitype, Portland, Oregon

Library of Congress Catalogue Card Number: 82-72079
International Standard Book Number: 0-910315-01-9

Printed in the United States of America

Table of Contents

FOREWORD

This is a spiritual sex manual.
It is written by Jesus the Christ.
More than this you do not need to know.

The relevancy of this work shall be apparent only in its application to your most intimate aspects, how you feel and think and know the Truth of these words within you.

It is not difficult, my children. Let me show you how:

First, acknowledge that I exist.

Next, acknowledge that I exist within you, for our minds are joined, and you are indeed my Brothers in God. We are all Sons of God.

Next, know that I AM, even now, that I did not "die," and that I exist within each of you as Guide and Counselor, Helper and Friend.

Now, erase all capital letters and know me in Truth as brother and guide and helper who would walk with you out of this world and to Heaven, not at the end of your lives, but now, in the wholeness that you are.

This is an introduction to one of the most famous books you will ever read, or ever hope to read. It is not famous because it addresses a universal need. It is famous because it addresses a universal illusion. You are all caught within its web. So be it. Let me help you out. If you choose sex to be that vehicle, I can help you. If you choose other means, I can help you. I am your helpmeet, so designated by God. What you choose, I shall develop as your way to Home and Heaven. To the return to your Source, shall I lead you. That is my Function. What indeed is yours? For each has his or her unique and special Function within God's Plan for the Salvation of the world.

How choose ye, my children?
How choose ye, scribe?
Is this the foreword of our book, or isn't it?

Jesus the Christ

To The Reader

As you go, my children, to consider this, our book, realize that the ending will be for you what you make of it, as will every page in-between. Consider for a moment that the importance of this work lies not between the covers of this book, but how its teachings are accepted and used by each of you.

Now consider as well that the subject which both fascinates and repels you is not to be taken lightly and as an adjunct activity. It is a vital and important part of your total life, and not to be regarded as dispensable. Those energies, those sexual energies, are one with the God-energy of the universe, and when blocked and abated, when repressed and denied, will surely fill up the dam of ego and cause untold misery within you, both physically and mentally.

Therefore listen well and read well. Know that this book holds the key to a new dimension of sexuality in your lives. Know also that the scribe of this book holds no claim to recognition in the work she has done. This is not a denial of her contribution in allowing the book to come through her, but it is a disclaimer of her as author, and it is a disclaimer of her as one who comes in any special way. See her as One with you. That is all. That is my commandment to her and to you.

Unfold now, in the pages that follow, a new concept of Jesus the Christ. See me as contemporary in your world; as close as a whisper in the ear, a tremor of the heart; a loving hand held out to yours as you go to be with me in this New Age of Aquarius.

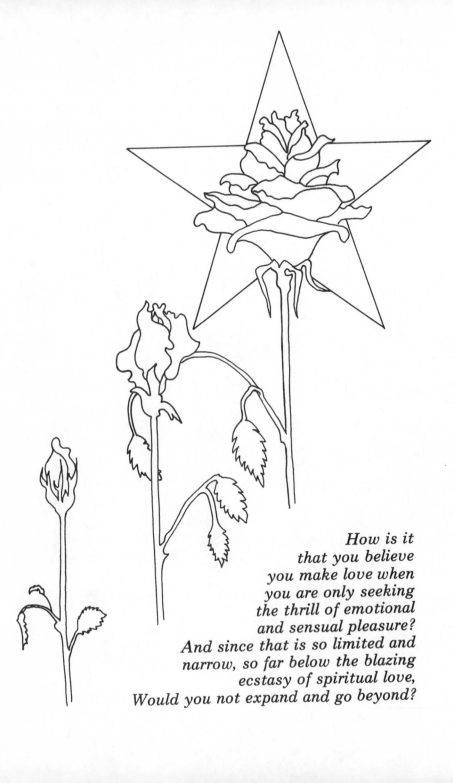

How is it
that you believe
you make love when
you are only seeking
the thrill of emotional
and sensual pleasure?
And since that is so limited and
narrow, so far below the blazing
ecstasy of spiritual love,
Would you not expand and go beyond?

Chapter 1

Foremost Among Them Is Love

Let me take you by the hand and tell you a story, my children. It is not a happy story, but let it suffice to be for you a lesson in avoidance, for no one could possibly want to have such an outcome in their lives, but so be it . . . the choice is yours.

Surreptitiously they came into the darkened room, hearts aflame with excitement and anticipation, trembling in the half-naked state which was soon made complete, gently stripping each other's bodies in the warm half-light, becoming ever more stimulated at the ripening view of contours of flesh, and the revealing of the physical intimacy between them . . .

It is a familiar enough beginning, is it not? Have you not experienced such a feeling, a similar situation? And yet, what is missing? What is the ingredient which can transform this physical and emotional linkup into the radiance of pure bliss, of true Love, of the linkage of God into the experience, a contact which can create an ecstasy beyond anything the mind-body can design by itself?

Tenderly they came to close the gap between them, to finalize their love in a blazing moment of joining. Closer and closer they came in their passion, hoping to end the inner emptiness, the faulty perception which told them that they were separate, alone in the universe, with only certain special people there to transform the terror of separateness into the warm flow of joining. Surreptitious moments, the illusion of having bodies join, as if in that joining more were really possible . . . somehow. And the bodies connected, melting in the great wave of pleasure and tumescence and carrying them into an individual experience of ecstasy . . .

"Not bad," you say? "What's wrong with that?" My children, again you cannot know until you have gone beyond. You cannot know there is something more if somewhere, somehow, it is not communicated by those outside your thought system, or by some inner impulse that sends you seeking beyond the empty pleasures of the moment that make no bridge, that make no true joining. "It is enough," you say? How do you know?

The two standing by the window afterward knew it was not enough. They knew the emptiness . . . the casual encounter that promised so much gave only titillation, temporary closeness, and now the seeming love was gone, the indifference and emptiness returned, the ending of the dream of union was once more over, and the loneliness had begun again. Separate people in separate bodies . . . nothing more . . . nothing less. An eternity of separateness, until somehow death would come to take away all that had been given.

They knew themselves only as bodies, as feelings within those bodies, as minds within those bodies, encased in littleness. How could they know the true extent of their Beings without being afraid, without the fear of being carried into such vast change as to terrorize them? How could they reach out for something more, unless they knew they were Something More?

And you are, my children. You are all Something More. I am Jesus the Christ, come to speak through this scribe on a matter of such great intimacy and sensitivity as to send the world scurrying to its weapons. Jesus? Write on such a subject? *Impossible!* Was He not without sexual needs? Or did He not master those lowly needs, those body needs, so that He rose again from the quick and the dead, and came to us to demonstrate that somehow those needs were lowly and full of stain and shame?

My children, you know not me. I am your brother. I am not a special God placed above you. I am within you. I am One with you. You ken not Who You are.

But *I* know. *I* know. And I come to you now asking you to come together in a new way. A New Age is emerging on the earth and the old is changing rapidly . . . how rapidly you cannot know. The subterranean movements of reconstruction are going about their business so effectively, so powerfully, that nothing can stand against it, and God is pleased, my children. His Workers do well. No destruction is being presaged for its own sake, only change that will bring peace and joy back to my children.

"Jesus the Christ," you say, laughing? *"Jesus?"* And the laughter abounding trails off into a tinge of awe.

"But what if . . . *What if it's true?* Then what? Ought I read on? Is it a sin? Would I be condemned by the Father to everlasting hell if I read this book? Or if not to hell . . . is it a snare for moneymaking, a stunt to sell books? Oh sure, that's what it is. Has to be."

God has no need of money, my children. He comes to you in this book, knowing that the furor which will reverberate to the heavens is not real, and cannot harm anyone. This scribe has no need of money through this book, for she knows her natural inheritance is abundance, and that from God. Be at peace, my children, and listen.

Decry not, my Brothers, the timing and the scope of this work, and the assignation of my mind and thought and personality to it. It is not mete that you judge at this time its purpose and its scope. Ye ken not the activities of God in this, the new Age of Aquarius. Many things will no longer remain as once they were in the sacrosanct caverns of ego, for the thinking of the world, even the religious thinking, the "spiritual" acts of Jesus are no longer to be looked at as "gospel", for the distortions of the centuries have so overlaid his words and his teachings that a complete cleansing of the temple is now underway to begin anew his Work on earth.

The Work is to go forward now in a new way, and this book represents one of those ways. Be about now the unveiling of all that would hide you from the truth of what you are, and of all that can be part of your experience in this, your life on earth. Ye ken not, my children, the import of this book and all that is happening to grace your lives through it. Judge it not. There is only learning to be accomplished. Let us be about it now!

It is time to be totally honest with me and to tell me of your experience in sex. Are you really comfortable in telling me that you "make love?" Aside from the fact that you *are* Love, how is it that you believe you make love when you are only seeking the thrill of emotional and sensual pleasure? And since that is so limited and narrow, so far below the blazing ecstasy of spiritual love, would you not expand and go beyond? Would you not seek out under my guidance all that is possible for you?

Sex is not sin. It is an illusion. But Love is not. Learn from me how to place sex into a truly loving context. Learn from me specific techniques . . . yes, "how-to's" in the act of *love sharing* that will transform it into an experience of holiness and blending in which nothing is lost, no uniqueness is sacrificed, no individuality given up, but rapture and Love brought to its own height and level of Oneness.

Is it not time that you learned who you really are? And is that to be feared, when Love is part of that experience?

Gently, gently, we go, my children. I would not push you, nor lie to you, nor give you false hope. We go to God together, in readiness, in Love, in the single moment of Truth that tells you you are immortal, invulnerable, and intact in the Arms of God.

The Divinity within each one of you is Real. Nothing else is real. Keep ever attuned to this. It may not be true for you now, but hold to it and let me demonstrate its truth to you. All that you need do is to be willing. Nothing more. I will not catapult you into an experience of fear. I will lead you sensitively into an experience of perfect fulfillment, and yes, through sex.

Let each one come to me now in the innermost place you can find. Close your eyes and be free of the shadows of the world around you. Turn to the inner spaces and talk to me about this book. Let me tell you about its efficacy . . . how it will work in your life, and that . . . yes, it is all right, my children . . .

*God hereby gives
you permission
to read this book.*

Consider, my children, the lilies of the field . . . absorb into your minds all the nutrients of the soil of the Spiritual Sex Manual. Let the words, the ideas, the conceptual material, the techniques, all come to be a part of your every-day existence. It cannot be that you adopt a spiritual attitude just to be turned on like a faucet when you wish to "make love." The pull of your old conditioning is too strong. This is a commitment to being with me during your days *and* nights.

"And how," do you ask, "can I be with you, Jesus?"

You will find a hundred paths, nay, a thousand. Only give your permission for your Way to unfold before you and wait patiently for that certainty to come.

Only be sure that the choice is made with God. Leave yourself open to His guidance and talk to Him in your solitude . . . and then listen. In many forms it will come, the guidance . . . in strong inner tugs to certain action, in words that come to your inner ear, in messages that are given you in the speech and communications of others, in books of spiritual truth. The entire world around you can become a channel for communications from God, but it must be from within a firm center that you listen, from a silent, calm mind that accepts that it is One with its Creator, and attempts its best efforts to realize and remember that Oneness.

It can be easy. Only pace yourselves through your days and remember this:

The Identity of God within you can guide you safely through all questioning and doubting. The fruition of His Works within you will bring peace, and you will never-

*more question His Presence again. But this is all depen-
dent upon your participation, your cooperation, your willingness. You can delay as long as you want on this path,
but in the end all will come to the Truth. There is only
one Truth. How could it be otherwise?*

Confront the issue now. What is to be the theme of
this day? Are you willing to continue on? Or will you
judge and condemn and say, "God talks not like this to
man!"

Oh, but He does, my little one. He talks like this all
the time, and it is imperative that you realize that He is
a living God. He did not stop communicating with His
Sons in biblical times. He has continued and will continue, until the last voice of pain is stilled. This is His
commitment to you, His Son. How say *ye?*

A star has lighted the purple sky,
and it comes to earth whispering
of a shadowy love of long ago,
tremors, pulsations of ecstasy . . .

Chapter 2

Love Remembered

In the holy city of Galilee many years ago there lived a man whom many revered as leader of his chosen people. Little did they know how his Kingdom would descend upon earth, for their visions were of another kind, loftier, richer, more opulent and powerful than any kingdom ever known. More than all the riches of the Spirit did they revere the materiality of the kingdom. Even his own disciples did not understand.

But there was one who understood. Mary. Mary Magdalena. She knew, as few ever knew, the totality of the man called Jesus. Let me tell you about the story of Jesus and Mary, the one that no one else knows.

There was a field in Galilee where they used to meet . . . under the nightstars . . . and the images of that time and that man, they are still in your mind, are they not, my child? Mary . . . remember ye not? You were my "starchild" then as now . . . no different, only then we were both in physical body, and more than friends, even as now.

Mary. Remember now.

No one ever knew, and had they known, would never have suspected, that the world would come to worship the Jesus man and consider him as having lived a life of abstinence. That came later . . . a fantasy for ego reasons.

A star has lighted the purple sky, and it comes to earth whispering of a shadowy love of long ago . . . tremors . . . pulsations of ecstasy. You were brown then, my Mary, long-limbed and lithe, and faithful even as today. Even then you had made your choice in me, and there was no altering your heart.

The words come hard on the page. The fingers tremble to type. This is not new to you, you know that. Why not tell them, my child? Why not loose the love affair of the centuries? It is no different than so many others. I was no different from so many others . . . grounded in the earth and yet soaring perhaps a little higher than the rest of you could at the time. That is all. I am your Brother. I am your Beloved. I am not different from you in our native substance. We are *all* the Son of God.

Now you must put your heart a little back from its pounding, and listen. Long have been the days and nights since we were separated in time. Long have been the dusty centuries, as I have watched a false image of myself being hoisted into a shadow over the earth. The image is crumbling now. The time has come.

The old disappears. The new is taking form. Soon you will all come to see your own power and glory as God's Son, and the old questions will all be answered, even as this one is.

I was a man. I lived as a man. I ate as a man. I slept and worked as a man, and I knew women. Write, my child, write! . . . without hesitation! Mary! Did you not know when you agreed to come and write this book that it would not be easy, that to open the crumbling pages of history would make you tremble and be discomfitted?

He sat thoughtfully for a long while, elbow on his knee, resting his chin in his hand . . . then suddenly there were blue eyes looking at me, with a fierce, intense look, and I heard the words:

Mary, it's time. You were always mine, even as now. There is no difference. We write this book together to give the world a new view, a new way to see. They would never listen if we do not share our story. Even in this lifetime you have experienced me as man, if a somewhat less solid "man" than you are used to. Sweet, we have to tell them. The world allows so much pain to be perpetuated under the name of "making love" . . . would you not help to end that? It is like a seed we shall sow under the turf of civilization. This book will nourish the seed, and the minds of all who accept my teachings in this book will find for themselves the experience unfolding.

Have I not said that I would come again and receive you unto myself? Did I limit the ways in which I would come? Would you have me do so?

I come in all ways, and in your eyes, this is one of the most startling and unusual and perhaps . . . unsavory. That Jesus the Christ should choose to manifest this way . . . and on *this* subject! And who does she think *she* is, anyway?

I will tell you who she is, for she does not know herself, as yet. Ever daily does she struggle toward the realization of her own Divinity, even as most of you do. But her love for her God and for me has allowed one of the most unusual recorded events of all time to be shared with the world, and here it is that we tell you of the monumental work now in progress called Come No More to Altars of Nothingness.

Long ago a little child in another land asked me, "Jesus, sweet Jesus, what is the source of all the Love you pour upon us?" and I answered, "My little child, the end of all hate is the beginning of all Love. We must find the source of the hate and dispel it so that the Love which has always been there can find expression."

And she looked puzzled and asked, "Jesus, what is hate?" And I answered her with loving care as I said, "Child, it is a shadow laid for a moment upon the face of Love, and dims its radiance, even as a cloud across the moon."

It is for all of us to uncover the shadows, and let them float free into the nothingness that they really are, so that we may rediscover the meaning of Love and our Identity in that Love.

Abruptly hasten to the edge, my Mary, and peer over. The abyss is not a new place to you. You have hung here before, on a silver thread that looked as if it would break at any moment. You are once again at the abyss, and it is only your total trust in me that will carry you through this time. Write the words you hear. No more is requested of you now.

Mary, come no more to altars of nothingness. Come to me, as of old, as of old. There is no difference, and the experience will be no different. We are One, now as then, and the manifestation of the experience will be powerful, sure and shareable. That is what we are about now.

Come to accept your bodies
for their only true purpose.
They are vehicles for communication,
for the communication of Love.
That is their only purpose.
Give them no other,
and you will see a transformation in your lives
that will give you endless cause
for joyous celebration and gratitude.

Chapter 3

Innocence Restored

And they came, one by one, stealing in with show of bravado and worldliness. The ones who were in first stood silently by while the women were paraded before them, nervous, unable to smile, stiff and attentive. It was all new to them, this being with women in this way. No one had ever made it clear to them that there need be no shame in this, the participating with those in the oldest profession in the world. The young men who came to be initiated into this secret rite were frightened, repulsed, and yet somehow eager, for the love which was being displayed in the faces of some of the "lovelies" seemed fleetingly real, even a concern and caring for their apparent discomfort.

The time was long ago, when the world still made much of virginity, and yet, what was a young man to do? The societal modes were stiff and strict, purity was prime value, and the only way that sexual satisfaction could approvingly be had was with the ladies who came "that way."

There was, in these young women, some of them, a sense of loving, of fulfilling a need, or serving a purpose that somehow transcended the apparent, the obvious. The ending of the brief relationship was easy, and yet the good moments, whenever so briefly there flashed soul to soul . . . these were cherished in the mind, even if never spoken of, or shared with sisters. And sometimes sisters slept with sisters, tired of the mauling and broken, twisted actions of men who came cruelly and did not understand.

Shall we tell them now, my child, how it was with us? No . . . later, later, for first let us go to the conceptual . . . the seeming challenge of the "real."

The false accounting of guilt is the seeming biggest obstacle to the flow of love between man and woman, woman and woman, man and man. There is no projection quite so harmful to the being than to see oneself as a body, and then accuse that body of being sinful, that is, full of error so magnified as to become inexcusable in the eyes of the beholder.

"Sin" is that which seems to be unforgivable, made so by a mind that would tell itself that it is damned, not to the traditional fires of hell, but to the self-condemnatory fires of judgment and hatred. Some of the more conventional approaches to self-accusation take the form of hostility, criticism, defensiveness and attack, both verbal and physical, expressed or unexpressed. No time is to be lost in releasing all these many forms of self-hatred, my children, for now we come to a time and place where any negative expression will form in the mind a wall of darkness that will block the flow of the Light into your relationship.

Say these words often to yourself. Let them sink deeply into your mind and heart and become your own:

I forgive myself for all the acts which I have committed which seemed to bring pain to others and myself. I see the end of self-condemnation before me, for I allow myself to see my negative actions as only mistakes in my learning process, and forgive myself and others for all the errors which I have ever perceived.

I accept myself now as being beyond the body, yet within it, knowing that I am growing ever closer to realizing the Perfection Within. I see all others in this same way, and I am patient and tolerant, understanding and loving, as I go through my days and nights.

Let peace come now as we go to consider one of the most difficult of subjects, the societal condemnation of the bisexual or homosexual person. Here public prejudice and judgment flame to the heavens, for where is there greater sensitivity than in the matter of sex?

Come now, my children, and let us hear what it is really like to be a person practicing sexually deviant behavior in our society. It is not what you might think, for though the price is obvious enough in the condemnation and exiling that occur, what is the hidden pain? Is it not that buried deeply in the soul, covered over with layer upon layer of fear, is the belief that the deviation is a curse from God? Yes, even while the role is actively sought, there is a level upon which is experienced a cruel sense of separation, even for the most hardy and cynical. Separation from others in the essence of your being is impossible, but on the body level, here in this world, the seeming separation from others is experienced as painful, to one degree or another.

It is time to see that the sexual aberrations of others are not to be condemned and judged as unworthy and unclean. It is time to be aware that I am in no way judging you for the acts which are accomplished by you in this dream you call your life. Why should I waste my time with such things? I care about you, and wish to end the illusion of pain which besets you. But how can I tell you how empty and useless are the longings for vengeance upon your Brothers that you create, and how totally without substance are the acts that you call "sins"?

The erosions of the Perfection of God's Son are illusory. No more are you to call a person by the name of "sinner" and no more are you to call sex a "sin" under any condition. There is no sin, my children . . . not that I give permission for you to run rampant in the streets, murdering and looting and raping and pillaging. It is simply that when you come to complete Clarity in your understanding of the meaning of the word, "sin," you will be *unable* to harm another, *literally unable.*

The illusory nature of the perspective from which you now see must be altered to include Reality. When this is accomplished, there will be no more conditional loving, no more spreading thin the illusion of caring. Let there be Light upon this matter, and let it be done in depth in my other books.

God blesses His Sons, no matter where they think they are, or what they think they are doing. He only calls from the depths of His goodness, reminding you that you are One with Him. Where then is there an opportunity for sin to become *real? It is impossible, do you not see?*

Much has been perpetuated in the name of Jesus the Christ. Do not go forth from this book saying that I advocate prostitution and pornography, homosexuality and sadism. I do not. But in my love for each of you, in my caring for each soul that is Brother to me, I offer my comfort and my help. Others may say that I call certain actions, "sins." Now you know that there is no sin.

The ladies slept lightly on the nights that Jesus came. His gentle touch and healing manner, even as he laid with them, transformed them into angelic beings, and they found themselves transported into new realms of love and delight. His Ways were man's ways then, and he knew that to be as man was the only way he could ever save his world. It is no different now. In proclaiming his manhood with them could he come to give them hope and succor in a time and age when they were devalued and deformed in their minds by the limits of their profession.

It is there that I first met you, Mary, and knew you. You do not remember? Transpose yourself now into that time, and know that the bed we shared then was warm and comfortable and of exquisite beauty, for the embroideries and the colors were your favorites then as now . . . the sweet burgundies in all their opulent shades. They are edging now into purple in this lifetime, as you grow into your full spiritual stature . . . but then as now, the burgundy tones were yours, and you wore them well. Flowing garments were your delight, and you spent much time in bringing together the most beautiful and unusual of tones and textures. Was it so different then, my child, you ask?

Yes, my Mary, it was different. You cannot remember, but I can. My mind has a perfect record of that time, and everything that happened. You experience your record as through a glass, darkly, and the images are faint. Mine are not. They have perfect clarity, even as you think you see your world now with perfect clarity. It is not so. We leave that story for another time.

Mary, write this now . . . the "how-to" section of this book is but a re-creation of that time so long ago, and as you move with me in your marital bed, you but repeat with me what you learned then. We shall share it all.

The next part of this book will be designed to lead you to Me, My Children. This is your Father speaking.

The full import of this revolutionary Work will only become apparent long after this scribe is gone from this body. She must have faith now as she writes that this was done for her Father, according to His Will and her Own.

My Children, were We, Jesus and I, to leave this subject of sex unattended by the clearing Light of Truth, We could not have this world be healed of its torturous ways of pain. When you clearly and completely understand the workings of the ego mind, the "stranger within," then you will see with perfect clarity how important is the Work being done here.

Read with open mind, and My Blessing upon your souls. I created you in Perfection, in Beauty and Light, and to accept less is to deny yourselves. I rest content in the future development that is to come, in the liberation of your minds from the body level of identification, and the pure and certain knowledge that you will awaken in My Arms one day.

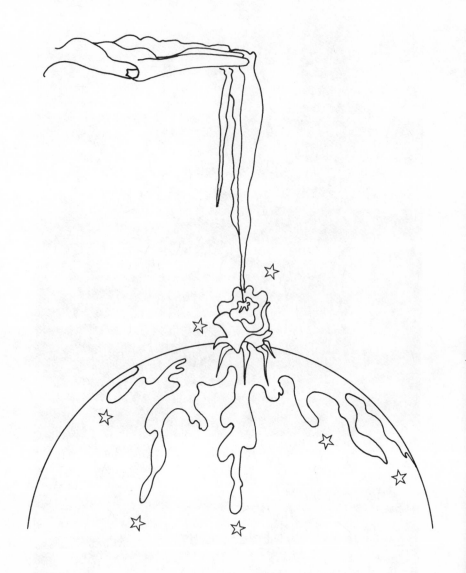

Purification is necessary first. This need not be experienced as painful. Only you can ask for pain. Do not.

Simply *see* . . . ever more clearly, that all that is before you is illusion, and transcend it. It does not mean that you must annihilate or punish your bodies. It simply means that you come to accept them for their only true purpose. They are vehicles for communication, for the communication of love. That is their only purpose. Give them no other, and you will see a transformation in your lives that will give you endless cause for joyous celebration and gratitude.

Mary, my sweet, come to me now. Let me hold you close. You but type the words you hear, and these words have not come easy. Come and rest.

"Jesus, help me please to put my mind at rest about this scribing. You say we are co-creating the book, that you are using my mind, that this is not a pre-written book like some of the others, that dictation is not a part of this channeling process."

"My child, be at peace. Many are the times I have dictated to you, so rapidly you could scarce keep up, when your mind was seized and seeming helpless to the rapid inflow of words and images. It is not so now. This is a co-created book which means that you and I write together, although I choose the words. I use your mind, I need your mind, I need your willingness to do this. Other parts of the book will be different. Right now we need this form in this way. You must be patient and trust me. I am coming to you in this form because it is the perfect form in which to communicate what we have to say.

"Come to me in meditation now and rest your body. The tension of your wondering has become uncomfortable for you. This, my child, has to be a believable book. Who would believe that Jesus the Christ could possibly know anything about sex in human body? Well, he does, love, and well you know, and we shall share it all. The old images of what I am are scattered in the dust of Come No More to Altars of Nothingness *and this book. The hue and cry will not be easy, except for you who are well trained in the projected advent of this book to the world.*

"You must trust me and accept that everything I do in this writing is exactly as it should be. We will make changes occasionally, fill in, alter slightly, but the human flavor is essential, child. Would you have a being from another world come to be in your bed, if you did not love and trust him? Well, so it is for our readers, who will find this dialogue in the book. Be at peace with this. Your willingness to be transparent in the writing of this book is absolutely necessary."

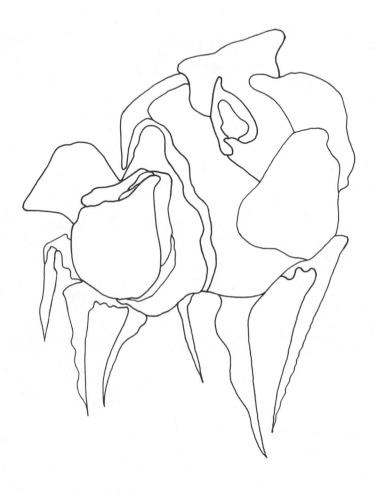

When you only communicate Love with the body,
what can it be but uniquely beautiful, tracing
patterns of exquisite fervor in every motion?

Chapter 4

Each One is Beautiful

Let us gather round, my children, this marital bed tonight, and see how gently, how lovingly, the Hand of God is laid upon it. Within each of you is the Light of Truth, of soul-energy. You can experience this Light and know its power to heal and to love, for it is Healing and it is Love.

Separate yourselves now from your body's eyes for a moment. Close them and clearly see the figure before you . . . it is a Being of radiant white Light, unsurpassed in beauty, in perfection. All hold this beauty . . . even you, my child, even you . . . as you look down at a body that may be less than beautiful in the world's eyes . . . overweight perhaps, slack and limp with disuse, scarred and distorted with time, imperfect according to the ego's standards.

Do you not know that the ego lives by comparison, and keeps you in chains by the mental act of constantly comparing body with body, nose with nose, breasts with breasts, penis with penis, face with face? When you stop playing its game and look at your body with only love, you will find that one of your greatest burdens can lift.

Many are the times when the best that is within you has yearned for expression, has coveted the creative joy of others. But in the act of universality, the act of sex, have we neglected the concept of beauty almost entirely. Oh, you have seen beauty in the bodies of others. That is so. But have you not neglected the shadings of the ethereal, the "seeing" of the Truth of what you are, as expressed in the grace and tenderness and majesty of your true Identity?

Say these words as you begin this reading now:

I, _____, do hereby give permission for a new perception of my body to occur. I understand that the body will not change; only the way in which I see it will alter. I choose for the ending of fear, and the beginning of a new Wave of Love to be expressed through me.

I choose for lovingness in every thought and act and word, and know though perfection be not available immediately, that it will come, and I will be free of those negative acts and feelings which cause so much difficulty in my relationships with others.

No more will I come to the act of sex feeling inadequate and bumbling, ugly and unappeased, because of the criticism of my ego mind. No more will I condemn my body for not being as I would have it be, for I realize that the ideal I have set for it does not exist, and is but a shadow I pursue in mistaken fumblings along the Way.

I accept you, my body, as the wonderful communication instrument that you are, and choose to see you as beautiful, for all the old comparisons are gone now. I judge you no more, and find you wanting. I am at peace.

When you only communicate love with the body, what can it be but uniquely beautiful, tracing patterns of exquisite fervor in every motion? Try it, my children. The Light is yours. I am not here to keep you in the shadows of envy and disgust regarding your body. I am here to restore the Light to you. When you give permission, you allow me to help you. Never despair over your body's appearance. There are ways to allow it to be in its natural beauty, when you allow it its natural function. Summarily, I come to be of assistance to you. This is one of my ways. Accept you it?

And now, standing full forth as what you really are, know this:

I am you. And yet, not you. And that is as it should be for right now, for this time in your life. You need to experience me as a Mind beyond yours, wiser, higher, more loving, more far-seeing. Tumultuous experiences have been yours in this life, and you cannot tell how it can be that I know them all, know all your pains and memories and joys.

Underlying all your fears and desires and passions, there lies another world. I am part of that world. I am also part of this world here with your conscious mind. I assume that the roles you are given here are perfect for you, for so they were fashioned in the Mind of God with your permission. You can choose how you will experience them. And yet the path of pain seems overlaid with necessity here and you do not understand. Let me tell you then, and the challenges of the God Plan and its

seeming demands will come clear as you see the Bless-
ings behind them all. Seeming difficulties come into your
lives, and yet you do not see that you have placed them
there, all of them. You do not see that you have chosen
them, and can re-choose.

I cannot teach you the depth of theory that would
make all this clear to you in this book. My other writings
tell the story clearly and completely, and I would have
you go to them, when this book is made a part of your
experience and your life. For by then will you know me,
and you will not be afraid to move on past the seeming
obstacles and crosses that line your path. As for now, we
have a bed to observe, and few are admitted that cannot
see how the mistakes of this union were perpetuated over
and over in anger and resentment and hostility for both
partners.

The end of travail is come clear in this marriage, but
there was a time when it was full of misunderstanding,
resentment, repulsion and frustration . . . even gleams
of hate. This scribe and her husband were participants in
such a marriage, and it is not easy for them to share
with you now those painful times. But knowing that they
only portrayed a universal theme with each other to
which many can relate, they have consented here to tell
of how it was with them before, and how my advent into
their lives and their marital bed changed everything for
them. It is the needed testimonial here. Be patient, my
children, and know that the ending of the book presages
a new life for you both.

Haltingly, full of resistance, and with no show of emo-
tion, she came. He, too, fearful and not understanding of
the release that was needed for them both. It was a

marital relationship bearing the burden of years of grievances stored in the mind and carried to the sexual act. Grudgingly they both came, though in the man's mind, the need was real enough and the desire excruciatingly sharp at times.

There was no foreplay. There was only an old, tired pattern of being together. There was no knowledge of the art of touch, of the unity between them. Manual manipulation, short, heavy gestures, dense and meaningless relating . . . the Light had almost gone out between them. Until one day, in an agony of being ground again and yet again upon the wheels of misery and despair, they turned to each other and asked for a better way. They asked the Holy Spirit to come and make their relationship holy. It happened once that the Light came into bed with them, but that was not enough. Many weeks and months went by, when slowly the lessons of forgiveness and loving communication and spirit identification were taught. The time was small in their minds for the Love that was growing somehow made it all worth the wait, even though often the old patterns would slip back in and both would feel the touch of despair.

That time is gone now. They live the works of this book. They are my testimonials, and we have only just begun. Let hope for you all come forth now. There is no marriage, no relationship that cannot come to this Altar and be healed. There is no other altar that can heal you. Come to mine and only mine.

Consider the lilies of the field . . .
how they spin not . . .
neither do they weave.
Weave no fabrications of shyness
nor ungentleness nor bluntness,
but in greatest tenderness
and loving abandon,
come to each other and explore
the mystery of God's Grace together.

Chapter 5

The Joining Of The Light

My children, as you go to bed with your spiritual partner, your Brother in Christ, be it man or woman, you are to remember but this and keep to it... your Oneness in each other and in me.

Be you ready to invite me to participate with you? Keep no stone unturned in your goal of willingness for this to happen, for in that willingness lies the answer to the whole mystery of what you are and what the universe is. To anticipate this experience is to destroy it, and so you walk a fine line, my children, in this.

Center your hearts now, one to another, and wait, quietly, in the inner silence. Feel the tiny pulse of excitement begin near the base of the sternum. That is the area of your spiritual flame, your spiritual joining. Then come to me for the words that will bring the whole process alive for you.

If you do not hear my voice directly, do this. Once you are at perfect peace and relaxation in your mutual embrace, place a finger on each other's sternum, at the base, and repeat these words:

I, a Holy Son of God, desire union with you on the level of spirit, as well as of body, and I ask you to consent to the joining with God which is possible for us.

Having spoken those words, gently press the base of the sternum with your finger. As you release the pressure of your finger, see the glow of white luminescent light that will be turned on with the releasing. Then the flame of the spirit, the tiny flame that nestles at the heart, will glow and grow in brightness, and leap across the imaginary wall of the body to join in a circle of Light that will reach out to encompass the Light of God which has come to join you in your spiritual union. See the three lights join in a beautiful white glow which fills the entire room.

And now, my children, invite me to enter your minds and guide and direct you to fulfillment . . . on every level. Have no expectations, one way or the other. Lie in the Silence, and let the Love of God permeate every limb and portion of the body, and let the loveplay begin.

Let the bodies be gently manipulated and massaged, especially in the hip area of the woman, but know that a woman's body has no special place of arousal, that all of woman's body is an arousal point.

Then let the nipples be taken between forefinger and thumb, ever so gently, and sweetly pulled and rubbed and turned. Let the forefinger press the nipple directly in with the lightest of touches. The resisting flesh will make its own delight. Let the back of the nails be dragged across the nipple with the lightness of a feather's touch . . . all so gently, so sensitively, that only the greatest ecstasy results. Let the imaginary milking of the breast begin, with fingers, with lips. Let the foreskin of the penis be gently pulled and that organ be lightly stroked. Let light movements of acceptance be made. The body will respond naturally and with complete abandon, if allowed to do so by the mind.

Let the joining of the Light be remembered in the midst of the ecstasy, and let no thoughts of guilt or sin enter into the purity of expression, for God would have His Children happy, and this is one of the modes of happiness in the illusion, once freed from the ego's treachery. Enjoy yourselves, my children. There is no sin. There is no guilt. It matters not whether you are with your husband or wife, or with another's, nor with those of the same sex. What matters only is your Love for each other and for God. That is all He recognizes.

If you have made a commitment to fidelity with another, then keep it. If you have not, know that no one owns you, and you are free to do as you wish. Keep your agreements, my children, while they are valid. If you do not wish to keep them, cancel them with the person with whom they were made. Be honest! Allow the ego no room for the twisting of guilt.

Not all can come to this, I know; not all can come to this in full readiness. Many will take these words for license. They are not meant to be. To incorporate the qualities of honesty and harmlessness, of gentleness and joy into one's life will bring about a natural extension into this kind of being with others. There will be no jealousy then, nor shame, nor reticence about any of this. There will only be open sharing. But without meaning and Love, without the Presence of God in the union, all will remain on the ego's level, and be twisted and turned and degraded into something less than Truth and less than happiness.

It is true for whatever you do. The Sons of God are misguided in their attacks on sexual activity as being of the "devil." It is only of the devil, or ego, when the goal of Truth and God is not introduced into it. So choose ye well, and know that the filmy veil which separates you from the Remembering of God is stretched across this experience as well as all your other experiences, and that these moments with another are powerful impulses into eternity. Use them well, in honesty and joy.

Now as for the moment of sexual activity which reigns supreme in the minds and bodies of men and women, do this . . . enter each other in the mind. Then embrace, knowing that the body is illusion, and that this mind-joining can greatly accelerate all that the physical joining is accomplishing for you. Penetrate with great significance to the plunge, and know that it is all of me and I AM God.

Have I not said that this is a practical teaching? Of what value is it if it deals not with affairs of everyday life, and what is more captivating to the mind in the illusion than the subject of sex? What runs our world? Look about you!

For God to leave this area untouched by His Teaching would leave ego rampant, and this cannot be. Be as little children in your innocence, and leave not one crumb to ego in your delight. "Screwing" . . . a word that torments the holiness of the act . . . be you invulnerable to it, as well as all the other degradations in your culture which obscure the true meaning and potentiality of the sexual experience.

Seek out the purity of the moment and let it shine through every act in your beds and elsewhere, when you are being embraced by another in sexual surrender. There is no difference, my children, for the sexual act can be an act of spirit, and the body but disguises that for those who cannot see. Let your spirits join and meld and flow together in this God act, and join with Him in conscious surrender of all that the ego holds most dear . . . the separateness that threatens every act of Love.

Consider the lilies of the field . . . how they spin not . . . neither do they weave. Weave no fabrications of shyness nor ungentleness nor bluntness, but in greatest tenderness and loving abandon, come to each other and explore the mystery of God's Grace together. Ask, and it shall be given; seek and ye shall find; knock, and it shall be opened unto you.

The spiritual joining shall be accomplished at a moment when you know not. Let each encounter be full and complete in itself, no matter whether the ultimate moment occurs in your awareness or not. Know that it does occur! And that each time brings you and your partner ever nearer to that ultimate moment . . . step by step, step by step, curving ever upwards to the lawns of Heaven. Be you about it now, my children. Jesus the Christ so calls upon you to let him join your sexual embrace, for so shall the true union of the spirit be accomplished, each in the other, for all eternity.

You make no eternal commitment by this . . . only complete and perfect fulfillment with the One. And how could that be obscene and profane? How, my children, how? You do not see Jesus the Christ in this role, and why not? Was I not a man as well, and did I not know my Mary? Of course I did. Let not the idealized version of what I am blind you to the truth. And what could be more ideal than to be a man in the fullest expression of Godhood?

Why should any part of your life in the illusion be unable to reach to Truth and to God? Why separate sex from that, and give it ego power? It has no power but what you give it, and what you give it is Love. In the physical joining is the Act of Love. Absent yourselves not from that act and pretend that Love is not there. Be you free and full and joined in the perfection of His delight . . . the true union of the soul.

"Jesus, I realize that this is only the first step, this chapter. Everything is different between my husband and I. You come to bridge the gap and join us. But what of those who do not bring their minds to be with you, who do not both welcome you together? What if only one person in the relationship is willing and knowledgeable and turned to spirit? Does it still work then? What can one person alone with you do?"

"Everything, my child. The power of God is unlimited, except in the making of choices in the minds of His Sons. Your will is free. But if there is only one attuned to me, the grace of That Presence can still be introduced into the relationship and the act. Surely the joy is increased if both are shooting for the stars together, but what does it matter, so long as you are experiencing love and peace? It does not take two in physical body, but it does take God and you together, you communicating with

Him and giving Him permission to enter the relationship and work His miracles. You have but to turn it over to Him in perfect understanding and release for the healing to be accomplished."

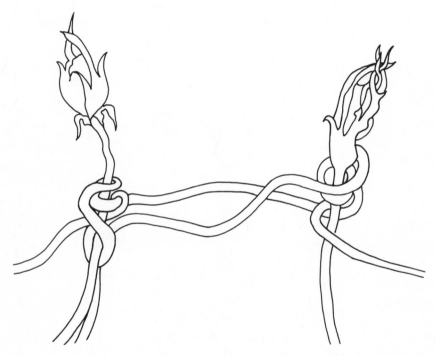

The problems of sex
are nothing more than a lack of Love,
and yet over and over and over,
the cries go up,
and Love is hard to express
in the midst of disfavor and resentment,
old furies and shackled feelings.
Nothingness blocks the way.

Chapter 6

The End Is The Beginning

Confusion has oft become the part of the Sons of God who have come to be with their Brothers on this sorry planet. They do not understand their roles nor do they understand that they, too, have come for their own Salvation as well as that of others. And they become spiteful and cruel to each other, and do not see the Love that is the base of their Being, one with another and linked only to God. But in the interim time that has transpired since earth became a planet of darkness, there has been a great revolution taking place, and the Light has come once more to be at home here in this lonely place, split asunder by the energies of evil.

You ask me what this has to do with A Spiritual Sex Manual, and I say to you that in no way can one's experience with sex be divorced from the total life experience, either the past or the present. It is best to see a gigantic amalgamation, a total synthesis at work here, and come to understand that the best place for sex is within a loving context.

So often women say that they are come to the sensual bed with feelings of tenderness and openness, only to be plucked like a chicken of all those transparencies of delight and love. Somewhere, somehow, there must a connection be made between the needs of men and the needs of women, disparate as they may seem.

Close enough to touch, and yet worlds apart! This is the cry that goes up over and over and over. The problems of sex are nothing more than a lack of love, and yet over and over and over, the cries go up, and love is hard to express in the midst of disfavor and resentment, old furies and shackled feelings.

Nothingness blocks the way, and yet it is seen as hardness and power . . . power of the mind to divulge only feelings of lust, power of the mind to allow only the animal-like sensations to be given expression, power of the mind to see only bodies, and nothing else. This is what must be overcome.

And the cry goes up, over and over and over, "Why will he not see what I am all about, and why will he not make some effort to understand, to learn?" And he says, "Most of what I need is being denied me. She only uses sex to get what she wants out of me, and she does not see my need." And so it goes on, night after lonely night.

The investment made in bodies becomes a major block to sharing Love. This much must be clear to you by now, for in this book it is our purpose to go beyond the body, to reach into the invisible, and to find that other part of the human being which is connected with the Divine and *is* Divine. This can only be done by a reaching and a choosing and a desire to go beyond, to find that which is the vehicle of immortality and to achieve union with it, as well as the physical.

Thus, your task is clear now . . . to begin to see with the inner mind's eye, and this is best facilitated with eyes closed and imagination bent as the twig in order to receive a higher level of experiencing and function. Rise above the physical body now, my children, and know that the ending of the travail in your life is not only possible, but is being called for now in the life Plan which you have chosen. This book has come to you not by accident, and in the choosing for its contents have you enlivened your sexual experience, and come a step closer on the spiritual path which you have chosen.

But in the experiencing, ever the temptation lies to fall more fully into body identification. This is not to be construed as evil, but only a mistake made by the mind due to past conditioning, You are not evil, but good, and evil acts are only perpetrated by minds who have chosen to listen to teachers who are of darkness, and not of Light and Love.

Chosen carefully are your divine Teachers. You chose them well before your birth and they linger carefully, and slowly do they unfold the Plan for your lifetime on earth. But in the interim of learning, do they often feel the temptation to chagrin and discouragement to see you unlistening and fearful and uncaring. This is not condemnation; this is reminding. See ever more clearly that the Ones Who come to assist you do know and have the power to change everything in your lives, but you are expected to do your part as well.

Evil cannot permeate a mind that holds itself closely to God. Know that as you move through your days, and as you read this book, listen well to the God Within that would move you into perfect synchronization with the life Plan which is built into your remembering. You are to be formed in this lifetime as a promulgator of Good, not evil, and you are to be considered as one with the angels upon completion of this life term.

Now the path lies clear before you, and once again we come to a part of this book which would lead you into a new experiencing of sex. But what of the blocks along the road, those areas of debris and danger and seeming fear from the past that would extend themselves into blocks of granite as you attempt to push past them? Invisible, yet impregnable . . . so they seem to you. But they are not, my children, and this aspect of our book will attempt to show you how to reach on past these interceptors in your divine growth. Come to see these things as illusion, as mirages upon the path, as miasmas of phantasy which would be as vaporous to the touch as mist upon the morning grass. And yet you cry out in despair as you confront these images of a revengeful past. Can you not see they are as nothing?

Fret not longer, but come now. Let us give them form and shape and name them, so that we may explore them one by one, touch them with the wand of Faith, and transform them into lessons of Love that dissipate the hard stones of the past.

*I come asking you to rise above
the battleground of the sexes,
to see the ground upon which
it is being fought as unreal,
and to transcend it in order to perceive
the Loveground that exists between you
in the depths of being.*

Chapter 7

The Battleground Of The Sexes

This chapter calls for much in the way of understanding and great sensitivity, for realize that no implications of inadequacy are real in any way here. Many factors go into the much maligned question of performance in the sexual area, but none are frigid, none are impotent in fact, for none are limited in the reality of what they are, and it is but mind that accepts illusions as Truth and calls the body to misalignment and dysfunction.

There now. Do you understand, my children, what I have just said? My blessings upon you now, for the pain which you have wreaked upon yourselves need not continue. I am asking you for a new perception of yourselves. There is nothing in the body which can halt the flow of Love, once the mind decides to lay down its mistaken perceptions. The body has no power to create, nor to block the feeling and the experience of sexual surrender. It has no power to do anything. We only give it that power with our minds, and can withdraw it at any time.

There can be many reasons for failure in sexual experiencing. We need not recount them all here. They have to do with the past, your personal past, and the false beliefs which have been engendered within you. We have only the present in which to create a new perception, and that can best be done by saying to yourselves:

I choose to release the past, and to see myself in a new way, as a Son of God, as Spirit, capable ultimately of all power in Heaven and on earth. If I cannot manifest this in my perception right now, I can at least grant that it might be possible, and start this day to loosen the chains that bind and limit my relating in this way.

Mind is magnificent in its ability to create and to dispel all that stands in the way of its freedom, and with the Helpmeet of God, the Holy Spirit, all that stands in the way of your perfect functioning can be undone. See it happening in your mind, but not without first requesting that "the stone be rolled away." The determination of your fulfillment is in your hands alone, and do not say that anyone or anything can stand in the way.

Accept these words for yourself:

I,_____, do hereby withdraw all power which I have given to other people or to situations to control my experience in all the areas of my life. I am victim no longer. I am in control of my experience, and by knowing this and choosing this, I start myself on the road to perfect peace and joyous fulfillment in all things.

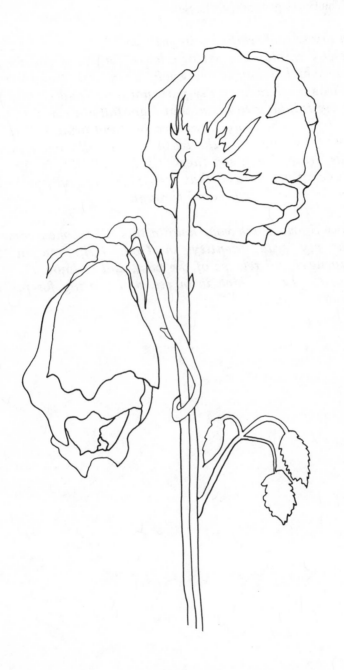

*In my sexual relationship with you, _____,
I hereby employ the act of release, forgiving you for the
blame which I have falsely laid upon you. I understand
this was a mistake on my part, not a sin, and simply correct my thinking to know that I am fully in control of my
experience. The more I practice this and bring it into my
daily living, the more the truth of this will come home to
me as Truth. I will say these words every day in full and
convincing measure so that their meaning and full importance in my life will come through.*

*Holy Spirit, I ask your help in this, that I may come to
know my true Identity in God. Help me in the
forgiveness and release of the past, and to know the depths of the Love which is in me, and waiting for full expression at last.*

MAN IMPOTENT

The man stirred under the blankets, slowly coming to consciousness of his surroundings, of the soft body pressed against him, the warm flesh, the leg draped over his, the arm resting gently upon his chest. He looked again. She was still there. She had stayed.

"Why, why?" he asked, "after last night! Why was she still there?" Despair filled the hollows and pockets of his body, a dull ache leading the throbbing of his heart. Why was it like that for him? Did she not see that he could give her nothing? *Nothing!* He was impotent. In spite of all her beauty and all her care, and the encouragement and the loving words, nothing happened between them that could bring her fulfillment, and he was cold and hard and angry and snapped the bedclothes back, bringing her awake with sudden fury.

"Gloria . . . get the hell out of here! *Get out!*" He spit the words, hating his body, himself and her . . . and then he remembered. Little intimations of his childhood came back . . . the teasing by the older sister and her playmates who had disrobed him in his tender years and laughed and prodded unmercifully to make him come to erection. Their tauntings still rang in his ears, and the words, "You'll never be able to do it! Ha, ha, ha, ha, ha, ha . . . ."

And later the fears that came when it was time to know women, girls, and still that stupid blocking of his manhood's expression when he wanted it so, and yet . . . buried deep in his mind . . .

Such meaningless events as that do it, my children. This is only one example from endless life stories . . . different in specifics, but similar in their ugly results. The effects of fear build in the mind, even after the particular event has been forgotten. They only surface as feelings of inadequacy and failure, and the mind, in believing the meaningless to be true, calls upon the body to act out its mistaken beliefs.

Beliefs can be changed, my children.

Paul wanted her. He wanted her desperately, achingly, his genitals throbbing, but still, still he was afraid. Why had she stayed after last night's flop? "Sure, she loves me. Sure . . . sure . . . but what good is that if I can't satisfy her . . . or anyone?"

"Take my hand, my child," he heard a Voice say. From within his mind came the words, faintly at first, then ever more clear, more distinct.

"Who *are* you?" he whispered to himself.

"Follow me. I will show you the way to be free of this pain," came the answer.

"Stroke her, my son, giving no thought to yourself. Stroke her arm, her thigh, not challengingly, but gently. Now flow Love out through your fingers. Start it as you would turn on a tap . . . see the Love Light flow as a stream through your mind, feel it course through your arm, your fingers, feel them tingle as the energy pours out upon her body.

"Now turn to her and see her as Light . . . no form at first, just beautiful, soft, white Light. Now a glow encompasses her body and forms a luminous light body all around the physical. You are that Light. You *are* her. There is no difference between you. Your reality is Light, also, and that Light is power to do all things. Say to the fear, 'Begone! You are nothing to do with me!' Let the Love Light circulate through her and back to you, streaming back as a warm and loving feeling, back into your body, enlarging its luminescence, as you mingle it with the feelings of Love and Oneness. It never fails, my son.

"When you stop seeing yourself as a physical body, and liken yourself to your true nature, all problems fall away. The false body identification that held you to that closure of energy is falling away now, as you release it by saying, 'I choose to let go of the fear that is gripping my penis, and keeping it flaccid and weak. I choose to let you go, fear that is nothingness, and charge you with love and appreciation, my body, to flow with this one who is One with me now.'

"That is all you need do, my son. The healing of this problem will come as a blessing of peace and Love, as do all of God's Gifts. There is no question of deserving. You cannot sleep with any woman without being free now. It is done."

Paul recovered from the transfixed wonder of his rapt attention to the Voice, and looked at Gloria. Her eyes were fixed upon him, wishing release for him, loving him beyond his sexual failures, wanting to help him with all the maternal loveliness of her being. She understood his need, and did not know how to help.

He reached for her with a joyous cry as his arms slid around her warm and naked body. "Gloria! Gloria!" Laughter and excitement slid out of them both as they felt the erection coming, and she rolled over with shining eyes and outstretched arms to receive him. The warm and joyous outpourings of their Love were melded into an exuberant cry of release as the stirrings of the God Impulse met and became One.

WOMAN ASLEEP

Recompense cannot be made, my children, for the ending of a love experience that comes not to fulfillment. "The woman, indeed! Is it not the man's responsibility to bring me to fulfillment? Is it not? The stupid oaf! He doesn't know anything!"

A familiar cry, you must admit. It resounds upon Heaven's ears every day and every night, in different languages, from all over the globe. Earth is not alone in being a planet of frustrations, but from Our Point of View Here it is by far the loudest in its hues and cries of malingering injustices.

And yet, my children . . . and yet, could you but see it from Heaven's Point of View, how different!

God, the Father, scratches His Head and says, "How can it be? I did not make My Creations imperfect and powerless. I did not make them to be victims of their world, but loving Co-creators with it and each other. What can We do to send them peace and the solution to their problems? Woman was not created as an helpmeet to man, but an equal partner!" And here we go again, getting into one of the more controversial subjects hovering over the heads of mankind, bespeaking derision and fear.

Resentment is fed into every pore of the woman's body, as she receives the man's fluent expression of consummation, and turns away in dry disgust and frustration. And he, feeling guilty for his own success and pleasure, quickly dresses and hurries away, wanting to see no more her accusing eyes and downcast mouth, feel-

ing her blame and condemnation descending like a drip-
ping mantle of hate around his shoulders. And his own
guilt adds to the pain . . .

So the ego would have you feel, my children. Paul and
Gloria are universal figures. So are these two. The
answer is not dissimilar, but different factors are involved, for the cultural differences in roles has to be played
out here.

Will you consent, my dear reader, to be the unfulfilled
one? Shall we give a gender name? Or not? What does it
matter? You are not your body in any event, but still, a
name would help. A unisexual name, perhaps? Kim?
Leslie? Why not? The matter exists in both sexes, don't
you see? Women do not have the edge here. But in
assuming passive and active roles, there the problem lies.

Why not make sex truly an interplay? In the giving is
the receiving. If there is no giving of pleasure, there is no
receiving of pleasure. If there is no sensitivity and
tenderness and understanding and empathy, if there is no
transcending of the body, then sexual play is limiting
and frustrating. In the woman's name is the woman's
game . . . nothing more. Let the woman play the man's
game, and receive as she gives! It is here that the Join-
ing becomes possible.

Ladies, you must give up your old roles in this as in
everything else. Why be victim? You are fully able to do
what God would have you do, and He would have you be
happy in all things. Read well this book. It has all
answers for any sexual problem within it. By following
these strictures, you will come to fulfillment, and know

that you and you alone are responsible for your frustration . . . no one else. Read on.

The anticipation of delight which serves to confuse so many regarding the act of sexual surrender is not a concern here in this section, my children, for my scribe only admits to an attitude of defection in this regard. She does not consider sex to be an act of delight in any way, and regales me with this fact at appropriate intervals.

Nevertheless, I persist, and she comes to see over and over and over that I am right in my devotion to her healing and her happiness. She is chagrined now to find these words appearing on the page, knowing that once again her God has triumphed over the ego in her, and is besting the negative influence that seems to keep her from fulfillment.

"Tell them, Mary, how it is with us . . . "

"Laughing and crying all the way, Jesus?"

"Now child, is it that difficult? . . . *(laughing)* . . . If it were not so palpable within her, this relationship with me, there would be much difficulty at this moment. No, my Mary has no problem with frigidity. She is easily capable of fulfillment during the sexual act, but look, little one, that is not true for many of your sisters, and I do not see any way to deal with this matter of woman's nature than through a woman. I need your help, love."

"To do what, exactly?"

"To give a woman's perspective on the whole situation of marital and non-marital sex . . . especially when a long-term relationship is involved, for it is here that most of the difficulty arises. The old grievances weigh heavily, and keep fulfillment waiting in the wings, anguished and frustrated, wringing its hands. Now is the time for you to share what you do know, for your marital relationship has been a challenge to you many a time . . . seemingly disparate personalities in conflict and misunderstanding.''

"Jesus, it is a very sensitive issue, you know that. Even while a woman accepts responsibility for her experience in the love act, nevertheless, there is the matter of physiology to deal with. The particular sensations evoked by the man's touch and actions can be experienced negatively, even when the man has every good intention. It *is* frustrating! At least I have experienced that when the man is touching, and does not understand how it is being experienced. It's like the old cliche of the violin and the master . . . the novice at the violin does not usually make beautiful music on the instrument. It is only when the touch is perfected and skill is gained that beauty of sound results.

"To me a woman's body is very much like that . . . mine is, anyway. Extremely sensitive to touch! Sometimes I experience incredible discomfort from a touch that is timed without understanding and executed without sensitivity, casually, without an observation or a 'tuning in' to where I, the whole person, am. Like . . . am I worried? Tense? Concentrating on a mental effort? Harried and rushed? At times like that, my body is like a tightly strung wire, and impact touch can send me into mental screaming. Am I speaking for all? I don't know. Is this what you wanted me to talk about?

"Jesus, even while I understand what you are teaching in the way of concepts about frigidity, there is still the question. To me, what the man does to the woman's body is tremendously important in producing the harmonious experience. How can the woman take total responsibility for what she is experiencing? Can you expect most of us to be able to control our physiological responses and experiences? I know ultimately it is possible, but how likely that most women can?"

"Hush, child, and listen. Your thinking is topsy-turvy and upside-down, and we go to right it for you and others this very day. Let go your concern and tune in now to a revolution in your thinking, for *know that your body's experiences and responses are determined by mind, and nothing else!* The body has no power to create, and the experiences you have while inhabiting it are created by the mind, and by your choices. Aye, the choices have not always been conscious and many have been implanted by 'race mind' and 'group mind' thinking. But nevertheless, it is ultimately a choice that rests with you and each woman as to how you experience the totality of the sexual act."

And shrieks rise across the land as Jesus the Christ is assailed by thousands of women protesting their innocence, and their freedom from such responsibility. For they do not see they are choosing that experience.

Did you hear me?

I say that if you are experiencing frigidity, you are choosing that experience, and can re-choose at any time, no matter what the skills and attitudes of the part-

ner . . . other than the actual giving of pain by that person, of actions of violence and bestiality.

In the "normal," the "average" relationship, the experience of frigidity is perfectly within the power of the woman to change, and it is this we are about to teach of now.

EROTIC FOREPLAY IS THE HEALING TOUCH

I am Jesus, come to give you the wisdom of the Universe in this regard. It may be different from all you thought before. It may be upsetting to you. It may give you disturbing sensations, mentally and physically ... or it may fit in perfectly with your present thinking. In any event, hear this:

Foreplay, as determined by the woman, is in direct line with all that she pleads, as she goes to foreclose on all situations in her life. There is never a time when she does not long for the romantic interlude, the endearing touch, the interplay with mind *and* body. Interplay that remains on the physical is only doing "half the job," so to speak. In this area of human experiencing, an energy flow that is limited and sparse cannot provide the full sexual experience, whether it be on a physical or a spiritual level, or both. Careless is the man quite often, when it comes to properly preparing the woman, and this is in no way negating my teaching regarding the responsibility of the woman.

It is an act of co-creation to which we go, and surely if the woman refuses to declare her dissatisfaction, and does not openly communicate so that the man can grasp the experience as she is receiving and creating it, then it is not possible for her to be fulfilled.

In communicating only Love, we do not stand pat on victimizing or being a victim. We ask all to go beyond such roles and to come to a place where true Creatorship can emerge into a fulfilling experience for both. Beguile but the mind without proper body stimulation and again you have a "half-assed" attempt at manipulation, not

Love. Once again, my scribe cringes at my choice of words, and once again, I patiently instruct you and her.

This book is for modern man. This book is for all men. This book is not only for the erudite. This book is for all.

Therefore as you go to it, expect to be "shocked." Expect that it is not going to fit your expectations. Expect that it will present things out of flavor with how most of you believe that things should be . . . especially things that come to you with the personality and the signature of Jesus the Christ. I will consistently break all the old idols! I will consistently use words and phrases to show you that I never left, that I have been in your world, participating and leavening the spirits of my Brothers as teacher, as leader, as guide. And it is no different now.

The true leavening goes on, on many levels, from many Minds joined to liberate the sleeping Sons who have decried my words as given before. The joined attempts to obliterate the Truth from them have well nigh succeeded, and only a few clear and clean minds still remain to give forth the unsullied works of Jesus from that time. That time is over.

I remain now, as I was then, outside of the expectations of my time. Generally speaking, mankind did not understand my Coming then, any more than he understands it now.

Bigotry and hatreds still flame across the land, and the "ingrates of Heaven" rise again and yet again to challenge institutionalized thinking. It is not limited only to those outside the church, my children, but there are revolutionaries *within* my organizations who work valiantly to scrape off the barnacles of two thousand years of unorganized growth and faulty interpretation. Only resign yourself to this: that the Truth of which I speak *will* come, and to each one of you. In time it will be shown that the labor of the centuries was not in vain, and permeated through all the errors of Christendom was the true, the blazing Light of God, protecting His Children from the many mistaken interpretations of the Teachings that have been perpetrated through time.

RISING INTO ONENESS AND PEACE

You are not to choose longer to be apart from your sexual partner. You are not to choose longer to separate and decry inadequacies in that person. You are to do naught but correct any mistakes that may be occurring by giving loving and open and honest communication. A flood of right thinking will inevitably occur . . . once the storm is bested. For you can expect one. There will be much defensiveness, perhaps, when first the gates are opened in a relationship where blocks to communication have been set high and wide between the two persons.

It is not mete that you allow those blocks to continue, to hide the grievances and pain and resentment and frustration longer. You must take courage in hand, and *communicate,* my children! I cannot help you unless you first take yourselves from your victim roles and choose to be what you truly are. You are a powerful spirit, one that can see clearly through the morass of negative thinking that has been built up between you, and one that can propagate right thinking in the relationship by loving, careful, *persistent* communication.

The body is neutral. The mind has power over its experiences while in the body. This is a fact not often recognized and almost never accepted by those in human form, but it is true.

It is why I felt no pain upon the cross. It was an acting out of . . . nothing, nothing at all.

It is possible to give up the need to feel pain, and that is all it is, nothing more than a need of the mind based upon the belief in guilt. How then could I, the holy and sinless Son of God, feel pain? And how is it that you can feel pain, being likewise holy and sinless? By your false belief does it happen in your experience . . . an illusion, nothing more.

There is never a time when you are not able to control your experience of your world. That is a potential in each of you that needs actualizing. But never in all the history of mankind has there been a sweeping attitude which would have produced a true belief in freedom from what seems to be the tyranny of the body. I came to teach that each man, each person in human form, has powers unlimited by appearance, that what I am and what you are extends in power and glory far beyond the world you know, and yet within it as well, within your experiencing of this world.

You take but infant steps now . . . each of you. Yet God watches and guards those steps even as an earthly parent encourages and assists and picks up the child when a fall occurs. You do not understand how much you are loved and protected and guarded from all mishap. And yet you do not understand that in the very power that you are given resides your seeming downfall. You expect that you are unable to be loving and unafraid, free of bodily concerns and the need to survive. I cannot help you when you are like that, for I cannot come in over the choices you make. You elect in your freewill choices that which you will serve and that which you will experience. I cannot do otherwise but follow behind that choice and give you hints and clues to choose again.

Everything follows from that choice you make, and it is well that you become aware of every choice, no matter how couched in fantasy and ambiguity, that you make.

You cannot keep your mind from making choices. It is happening constantly and automatically, unless you take charge of that process and keep your mind ever alert and ever keen to change those choices that are being made to your detriment. It is from this that lack and suffering and pain and death are born. You make them possible by your choices. That is the only way they can occur.

You are not yet actualized within your beings. You will be soon. Have I not said that a New Age is coming, and am I not a part of that New Age? My Teachings will triumph, even as I will triumph in the Second Coming which has now begun. I have waited long, my children . . . long have been the days of our seeming separation. Let the time not be long now before we are joined in your experiencing.

I have a world to save, and you with me. Come. The time is now. Let down your concerns for liberation based on bodily identification and come to know that in your spirit you are free, and in your spiritual choices reside your only true freedom.

Woman against man is not a choice for freedom. Spirit joined with spirit is. Would you hate your Brother because that soul has chosen a male body? Is that any basis for subsistence with the ego viewpoint? Why, my "lovelies," why? Is that term condescending to you? My scribe resisted writing it. Why, Mary, why? Do ye not ken that ye are all One in spirit, and that injustices done in this world are not real? Coming from power through attack does not bind and blend and harmonize and bring happiness. Surely you have learned that by now. No matter. We are here to bring together, not to split apart. Much good has come from a choice for freedom by women, and for better life conditions. I do not come to condemn that. But I do come asking you to rise above the battleground of the sexes, to see the ground upon which it is being fought as unreal, and to transcend it in order to perceive the Loveground that exists between you in the depths of being. That is what we are about here.

I could sing love songs of beauty and charm. What flutterings of the tongue could bring you peace? You must come to it in your own choice, not by truces in which you "fill each other's sexual needs," nor by compromises in which you go to your own sex to fill those needs, but to come to Oneness, where the only true peace lies.

It takes time. It takes learning. I am here to assist you. Use me. I come to deliver you from false and mistaken thinking. That is all that imprisons you . . . vapors . . . humors from the past . . . wisps of nothingness that break apart and fade away at the approach of the Light.

I approach you now. I come to you now, each of you, even as I come to her, for ye ken not that the Christ is in each, waiting for recognition, waiting for permission to be active, to take form in your thinking, in your life, in your experience. Call me what you will. I have no means to feel badly. I am past all that. I come to you freely and in Love, and perfect Invulnerability. And I *am* here. And ye ken me not.

Is it not true that you fear each other?
Is it not? For underneath the "love affair,"
underneath the appellations of love and contentment,
cold fear does swell, in its many forms . . .

Chapter 8

The Many Faces Of Fear

The foundation of fear within each mind has many forms of manifestation, but none is more intricate, nor shaded with guilt and pain than is the expression of the sexual relationship.

Now, be sure of this. There is no form of manifestation inherently sinful . . . because there is no sin. However, within the mind of man certain practices have come to be spoken of, and judged as, improper. Aye, some have been condemned as the worst of crimes. We but go to consider one aspect here that has found its place on the lighter side of the "condemnation spectrum." It has to do with oral sex.

My children, the term of manifestation is upon you. Will you continue to choose for the ending of the play of love, or will you take a new look at all that Love can bring you now? For if you do, you will find that there is no greater expression of Love than that which enhances the spiritual joining beyond the body. And yet, we use the body thus:

Place your legs, my beloved, in this position . . . rest upon pillows which support your back against a wall or straight hard surface. Then do this. Separate your legs widely, lean back slightly, but keep the upper body available to massage as well.

And you, my son, you keep all feelings of guilt and impropriety behind as you approach her, realizing that in this position is she vulnerable to every stimulation that you apply, and that in assuming this position is she demonstrating her supreme trust in you. Now, do this . . .

Massage the breasts lightly, the whole breast, and give no attention to the nipples now. Trace the roundness of the circle with your fingers, then close gently upon it as though it were a small, frightened little bird which you are trying to protect from a cold, rough wind . . . gently, gently go to close and warm and reassure. It is not maximal stimulation we are after here, but a "warm-up" . . . literally, a "warm-up."

Is it not true that you fear each other? Is it not? For underneath the love affair, underneath the appellations of love and contentment, cold fear does swell, in its many forms . . . fear of rejection, fear of being inadequate, or of being considered less than attractive, somehow not measuring up physically nor technically . . . not being "able to do the job," somehow or other. Usually these moments of abject fear are not shared, nor verbalized within, nor even noticed in surface awareness. It is part and parcel of a larger hidden mass of fear buried in the mind that surfaces to reveal itself, but which arouses so much discomfort that pretenses are made that everything is all right, perfect even! while anxiety pushes back wisps of distraught hair from the forehead, and whispers ever increasingly of torment coming, of loss and pain just around the corner . . . "Just wait!" . . .

The flutterings of the mind cease for a moment, and you remember my words, and you look at one another:

"Jesus says it's all right. I'm willing," are the words he hears, and he looks at her, smiling, grateful for his release from responsibility, as he continues to warm and caress and fondle.

And then he comes . . . straight to the area of greatest sensitivity between the legs . . . and knows, above all, knows that here is the greatest fear and here is the greatest pleasure, and he suspends his downward swoop in mid-flight. Here is he ever so careful, ever so gentle, as he alights with the butterfly kiss upon the mons veneris. Warm hands follow soon after, sliding the skin over the full, mounded hill, gently pulling the skin over the clitoris, stopping to rest and warm and tempt, then ever so slowly exploring with the fingers all the hills and valleys that lie like mysteries, inviting him with their cries of hunger.

Warm lips and tongue come soon and the woman is swooning, her upper body undulating to the rhythm of his hands upon her breasts, and his mouth upon her vulva, music slowly swelling and rising into crescendo after crescendo, as her body movements, rhyming with his, create new chords of sensation.

This old tired music-maker comes
   to a halt now.

Bereavements are never in order,

And the tip of the iceberg is about
   to come into view.

Will you not play upon it, my sweet, for he would love your gentle caress and the feel of your warm, moist lips gently sucking the tip of his penis, the feel of your warm fingers circling his groin and descending into rings of Love that slide up and down upon his organ. It is all right to put it into your mouth. God does not mind. Do it, and know the pleasure which it gives him, and the gift which you give, you will receive. And is it not pleasant to give ecstasy? Is it not?

Fill the room now with the soft and gentle sounds of your fucking, my children . . .

Why do you tremble so, scribe? Hush! Your world is not sensitive to that word. Why are you? Mary, Mary, I must get you out more!

Sucking the penis brings obvious delight, my little one, to your partner, and the end of the road together brings an explosion of ecstasy. Even so, many are obdurate and refuse admittance . . . either to mind or body. Such are you, when you refuse your mate the pleasures of sex. Do you not see how ego would set you up for guilt in this? Do you not?

Suppose that there were no such thing as sex. Would you still feel a source of guilt and shame about the body? And why would you? No one would be sharing bodies, or trying to. No one would be embodied!

You do not understand my words, and yet do you not see that without the sexual function and the overlays of ego upon it, bodies would be seen for what they truly are . . . communication channels? Peruse the pages of history and tell me of the role that sex has played in bringing pain and misery and guilt and jealousy to mankind. How can it be that the world would miss this painful aspect of its relating?

And yet they would, for some divine even here that it is a way to God, and search and search, yet they do not understand. It is a dimly sought hope, a way of relating to others that gives some promise of union, some aspect of Salvation that surely must be there. *It must be there!* But where? And how?

When you finally come to see this book in print and find its covers overlaid with blue and gold, as The Plan has chosen, you will find many who will come to it in suspicion and dismay. The joy that would bring peace and clarity will be kept from minds unopen to receive. The spiritual union will be bereft of its fulfillment.

The "birds of a feather who come to flock together" in spiritual sex groups will find a studious avoidance of the true meaning of this book. We do not come to talk of bodies . . . don't you see? And so long as you cling to the body as real, and cherish and involve yourself in it, so long will you be limited in the true fulfillment possible *through* it. It is in the "walking through" the body involvement that you will come to fruition, so give up your cherishing of the flesh as an object of passion, and reach beyond it to the true passion of the soul. And come to me, my children. Come to me.

Eyes may beleaguer you, and hands may grasp and stroke and knead and palpate, but never will you know God while you linger here. You cry out at the seeming paradox, I know. But it is possible to walk past and to meld the union into a tight experience of Perfection.

Come. See me shining through the mists of confusion that the ego would put before your intellect. You will not find me with it. I am beyond that also, in the inner peace which is my chamber and my Home. Come to me there.

Let go all thoughts of confusion and dismay and simply choose to be. Relax and watch your thoughts. Separate yourself from them. You are not them. As you do this, the body will relax and respond and bloom into a "something else" that is its true nature. You will find the God-essence in all things, even there, and it is this that will support you and gently clasp you in its arms, and carry you here . . . to me.

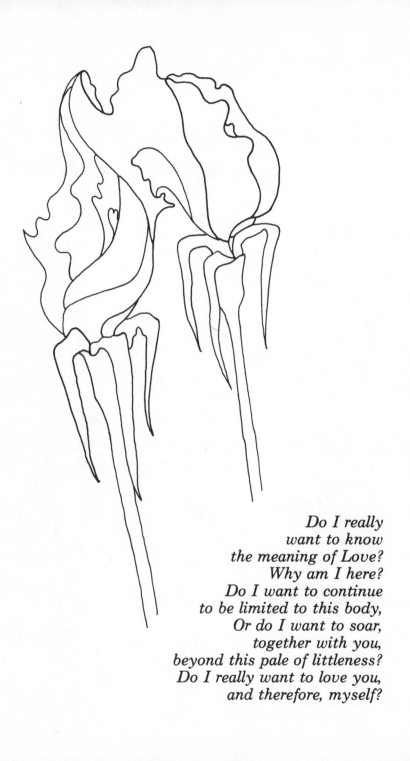

*Do I really
want to know
the meaning of Love?
Why am I here?
Do I want to continue
to be limited to this body,
Or do I want to soar,
together with you,
beyond this pale of littleness?
Do I really want to love you,
and therefore, myself?*

Chapter 9

An Act Of Love

It seems there is a hesitation in the mind of my beloved scribe, which is no way impairing the work, only detracting from her own joy. Now, my child, release your resistance and the tension that pulls at you. Relax. Let me take over and let the process give you that perfect ease and comfort which you would have. Come, Mary, and give me your mind and fingers.

There was no hesitation in her now as she heard the call that had resounded through her mind so often these past years. Since that first day he had come to her and without identifying himself by name, told her she would be writing books with him, so has she faithfully come, hour after hour, week after week, and now it has come to years . . . has it not, my child, years of being a scribe of Jesus the Christ? And has it been so difficult?

She will not answer you now, for no words could encompass her experience. Suffice it to be said now that herein lies a work of major import for her world and for herself, for never is a message only for others, but always first for the one who receives,and she is blessed now by what she gives.

But in that same vein, she knows well, and has been well trained to realize that any investment she makes in this or any work is to her own spiritual detriment. My training has been quite ruthless in this. She knows. Ask her.

Come to see the value in the personal dialogue between Mary and I in this book. It will help you to see my message in its true perspective, and to come to value and appreciate its content as reaching beyond this single aspect of your lives.

For in truth sex is but a single and not very important part of all that you hold dear, and to glorify it past its real meaning is the source of all your pain with it, my children. You see, you put it in place of me, your God. You put it in place of all that could release and liberate you. You make it your salvation, my children, and herein lies your pain.

But you would not have me remain in theory, I know. Come, let us go on to the "juicier stuff", for if it does not work for you, you will know that I am a fake, right? And it will provide tantalizing reading, that I assure you.

But it will not work for you if you do not come from the heart with it, my children. You must want to transcend the body. You must want to go beyond the experience you are now having. You must want something more, something better than the emptiness you now have. Otherwise you are not ready, and it will not work for you. Do not let my words disturb you. Simply be open and read and listen and be willing to try this better Way. That is all.

Mary, my sweet, it is imperative that they come to understand that you and I were able to do this together, and let it be known to our readers that you and I will share an accounting of this experience before the book ends.

The sections which follow are "how-to" pages. They are practical steps which you may use to visualize and learn the processes of spiritual sex. They are not meant as a recipe, once they are learned. The way will be opened for you to inflow the creativity of the Universe into your love-giving, so that each time will be new and fresh and different and unlike any experience before or after. It is the originality of your own creative beings which will be unfolding, and lending to the present moment its own beauty and warmth and excitement.

As for now, simply do this. Hold the hand of your loved one, and join with that one in repeating these words in unison:

I, _____, do hereby consent that our joining shall be of God and with God.

Stay a little in the silence. Let your daily thoughts fall away and ask for Silence to come. Relax your bodies, and let you take turns reading now the material that is to come . . . together, if that is possible. If you are alone, read on with me. I will come to join you at a single call. Now, let these words be spoken:

I choose to see you as you really are, beyond the body and in the Light. I see you now covered with sparkling white Light, and see you as I am . . . perfect, loving and truthful. Gentleness and consideration are my Path. I will not be afraid, but trust in the Love that enfolds us now.

Let the gentle initiatory embrace begin. Let it be asexual, loving, warm, conciliatory if conflict has lately been between you. Let the genuine need which you feel to come from spirit be the emotion that motivates you to close attention. Do not, in your excitement, fly on past all that would prolong your ecstasy and lead you to the goal of spiritual fulfillment. It requires careful pacing.

I have set before you, in the words that follow, a most explicit and detailed accounting of an Act of Love. It is written in instructional form, and it is for *you*. I come with the book, my children. It is an extra bonus . . . a built-in, live-in Teacher, and it is thus that I would have you see me now.

Lest you, my beloved, begin to fall in love with me as man, know that it is quite useless, for I am impervious to all such innuendoes, now as before. It is another call which comes to you now from me. I call upon you to walk with me through this experience, and come to know me as part of you, even while I am myself. And as you follow these complete instructions, know that you are partaking of one of the most divine of sacramental acts. The old conditioning must be let go, my children. It has no place here. Give all such thoughts to me, and that will tell me that in truth you would be with me.

Simply explore your friendship now. If you insist upon seeing sexual roles and expressing them, let the overtures be minimal and light. Mostly let it be a closeness of bodies, of minds, of thoughts as you hold this book on your laps and close your hands together over it, in loving commitment to its teachings and its truths.

And when a feeling of Oneness has begun to creep into the edges of your minds, then know this:

> *I come to each of you now.*
> *Invite me to enter.*
> *Allow me access to your inner beings.*
> *We are all the Anointed One.*
> *Let this be your reality now as you read.*

The Anointed One would find Its Presence warmed and enlivened by immersion in water. But before we go, my children, to this, I would have you in close and loving embrace, and this requires your total attention. Seek silence in your environment if it is available. Search within for that small point of peace which a relaxed body and quiet mind will give. Close your eyes, be comfortable and wear only your willingness to be open to my direction. Speak your permission with these words:

> *I give you permission, _____* *
> *to enter our relationship in full and complete freedom.*
> *Only you, _____, and no other,*
> *has this permission.*

Let fear fall away as you center yourself in the relaxation and peace of the moment. Enter each other's arms in warm and clear recognition of the spirit reality within each of you. Declare it thus:

---

* You may use my name, or that of the Holy Spirit, or a name of your own choosing to represent Divinity.

I welcome you,
into the God Triad which we form
by our joining together.

I see you as Light,
not flesh.

I see you
beyond the appearances of the body.
I see you as One with me.

Let the moment swell into a deep appreciation of each other, letting go of the negative emotions that may try to rise and block the flow of love. Disperse them as shadows without substance.

In the joining as it comes initially, realize that the most sensitive of inroads is in order. A gentle attuning must take place so that all the energy flows within the being are drawn into contactual affinity. Do not strain nor need you feel it necessary to *do* anything. Simply be . . . together. In the flow of pleasant annhilation which follows, in which you place your attention ever more clearly on the present moment environment both within and without, know that you are preparing the groundwork. It is delicious in itself when done properly. Allow God His timing in bringing you together. You will know when He moves you. Be willing to be moved.

Certainty will come as this gentle, loving overturing becomes a more or less regular part of your being together. It cannot be said that God sets up rituals, for no form can contain me.

Let it only be clear to you that you are both loved and loving. Look into each other's eyes fully and openly when it is comfortable to do so. Laugh, cry, be sad, if it helps to clear the way, but do not linger in it. A momentary tear of joy is quite acceptable. For you are coming together in a new way now, and you are no longer alone, "just the two of you." I have been given admittance to your relationship and it will never be the same again. Slowly . . . quickly . . . the choice is yours, but in the end, you all will come to this, to find the joy that is hidden in this communication between minds, souls, bodies.

The words are simple. You have said them many times, no doubt.

I love you

These are my words to you. Let them be now your words to each other.

Go now, if you can, to a scented bath or shower experience. If this is not possible, read on. If a shared water experience is chosen, let it be that the love between you is expressed in the same manner as the initial embracing in this chapter. Do not push for sexual arousal now. Let it be light and loving and warm . . . nothing more, but also nothing less.

Be at peace. Gather peace to you, as you would gather into your arms the bubbles of foam on top of the water which embraces you. Hold out your arms to peace and Love and feel them fill you. It will be an important part of the preparation on our path to ecstasy.

As you come together now, in a setting of your own choosing, let it be that you are attuned . . . whether the space be your own or another's, whether it be the ideal environment, or a drafty bed with harsh blankets, it will not matter. Simply free yourself of external concerns and focus your mind, each on the other, and once again repeat the words from the beginning:

I welcome you, _____, *into the God Triad which we form by our joining together. I see you as Light, not flesh. I see you beyond the appearances of the body. I see you as One with me.*

Embrace now. Slowly come together. Let the pressing of flesh upon flesh be sensitive and careful. Let the full sensation come to you, but hold ever in mind the true focus of your attention in yourself and the other . . . the spiritual center within. And let us begin . . .

Forefinger strokings are of great sensitivity in the art of touch. Couple that with the Love flowing from the mind, and you have an act of exquisite tenderness. *Keep ever in mind that you are spirit, acting through body and mind, that you are giving Gifts from God to each other in the form of loving communication.* This cannot be stressed often enough. You are actually sharing with each other the gift of what you are, which is Love. See beyond the body, see beyond this world, keep ever before you the illusory nature of this level of reality, for it in fact has no substance, no matter how solid it seems to you. It is but a dream. Transform the dream now into an Act of Love, and watch the miracles flow from your fingertips.

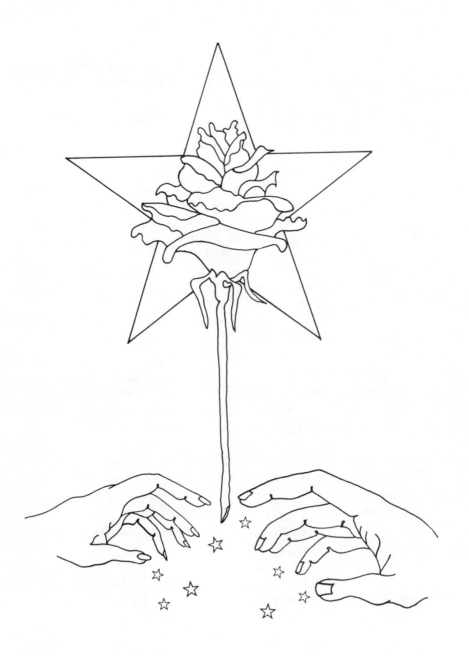

Press the nipple with forefinger and thumb as I have instructed you, my son, and let your touch be light and loving, and let her know as you go how much you are enjoying this gift which you are giving to her. It is not mete that you seek only the body sensations, but ask at every step for the innermost self of the woman to express itself. Keep ever mindful that you are communicating Love and only that . . . not possessiveness, not animal pleasure, nor insensitivity to her needs. Let her respond in like way to you, for the needs of both are the same in this regard. Let the foreskin be gently pulled and pushed back and forth with loving caress. Let the love flow from your fingertips. Feel the God-energy pulsating from your *mind* as you go to gently and thoroughly bring your minds into alignment with all that is best and highest in you.

Let concern and caring for the other be your maximal enjoyment, beyond the body, beyond the excitement that the ego would claim for you as its goal. Transcend it into peace and shining stillness. Hold ever in mind that you hold within your arms, under your touch, a Being of Light . . . a shining, beautiful, radiant Being of Light.

You may find my words hard to accept, and even might occasionally wish to throw the book down in disgust. That is all right. Just do not forget to pick it up again and read on. It contains such gifts for you as would make the angels weep were they to be discarded.

Let me go on now, and scribe, be you with me in peace. I am come as a Light unto your world, my children, to help you to recognize the Light Within. All means will be used for this . . . *all* means, save those of pain.

Transcend now, my little ones. Ever so softly be attuned to every corner of your entire bodies. See the Light-energy gently swirling around and into every nook and cranny of what you take to be your being. Be aware of it all, and let that attention now extend beyond your body to the body of the Other. Let it be that you see that Other in the same way, and when that act of attention is complete, that same swirling, gentle, soft light seen within the other person, then go on to see yourselves at One with everything in your environment, letting the light fill the room.

You are pressing each other close now, looking into each other's eyes with a wondering, beginning to know. Let me tell you now of each step that you must undertake. Slowly, sensitively, unfold the mantle of self so that what you really are can emerge for both of you. It is not hard. How can it be hard to be what you really are?

Hold me between you now in the area of the sternum. See me as a bright Light also, linking you, connecting you with each other and with God. See me as a transitional point in consciousness, helping you to be beyond the body. See me as you. See me within you. Let the Light that I am be seen in your minds as shining within you, between you, joining you in Love.

Now separate your bodies a few feet apart, and set your forefingers gently on the base of each other's sternum. Press gently and know you are pressing a button which is turning up the Light within you. Press firmly for an instant. Now turn the button, the imaginary rheostat, so that you are slowly turning the light ever brighter, ever higher. See the glow, the luminescence start to play a light game upon your bodies. See the joyous dancing of the sparks of light as they form coalescing patterns of movement. See the figures float and rise and fill the room with their happy patterns of movement.

They are rising and falling as swells of ocean now, and see each wave that breaks upon your bodies as sparkling with the purest, cleanest, whitest light you can imagine. The Light-foam from the waves is soft and warm. The Light-water washes lovingly, caressingly upon the two of you as you press together once again to form a Oneness, a joining that is now visible in your minds as a glow that envelops your bodies and makes you One. Lie basking in this delight for a few minutes . . .

Now I would have you rise upon the bed, upon your knees and face each other, hands at your sides. Simply look at each other, fully, knowingly, openly, not being ashamed to reveal all that you can of how you are feeling, what you are experiencing, sharing the Oneness that vibrates within you.

Now reach out. Press the other's shoulder with your fingers, and let the hand trail ever so sensitively down over each other's breast. Linger at the nipple ever so briefly and continue slowly, gently, down to the genital area. It is an exploration that you do, an opening, an unfolding of each other's flower. Let the fingers trace between the legs ever so lightly, not attempting to penetrate the most private areas. The building of the tension is delicious now, is it not? And the Love which is able to pour through your touch is being received by you as well from the Other.

> *There is no Other, my children.*
> *In Truth there is not.*
> *There is only One,*
> *And you are That.*

Facilitate the release of the body's demands now by once again embracing closely without attempting specific stimulation. I am One with you in this. Remember to call upon My Presence in your mind, not as man, but as the One Who links you with each other in Love.

> *Release now the ardor that is building,*
> *For I would not have you*
> *As a dam ready to burst.*
> *Frustration is not our intent here.*
> *Fulfillment is.*

What could the world not know
If it could only see that here,
And here only in Love,
Is everything it could ever want?

Nothing is withheld from you, my children, in this world, except what you withhold from yourselves. I withhold nothing from you now. In your joining is the joining of the universe. Know that. You are sharing your Love with *all* your Brothers in this Act of Sacrament. Sacred is the day. Profane attitudes have no place in this, our bed. God *is* here, and how could sacredness be gone?

Lie down again, and prepare to receive me into yourselves in your conscious awareness. Repeat these words, both together:

I, _____, do hereby give you,
_____,* as Emissary of God
come to heal us and make us whole, permission to enter
my body as Love, the Love of God come to save us.
Show me the way to be with my beloved in creativity; let
the Love flow consume us so that we no longer have a
way to feel separate and alone. I ask this in the Name of
God.

Wait silently for a moment, and then move toward each other . . . rather are *you moved* toward each other now, for you have given up your need to be in charge,

---

* You may use my name, or that of the Holy Spirit, or a name of your own choosing to represent Divinity.

and are allowing me to move you. And so I will. There are no patterns to be given now, for tumultuous movements may come, or slight movements so full of radiant feeling, so bursting with unfulfilled energy as to be magnified beyond belief.

Help me now . . . move with me now . . . there!
Let the storms come!
Let the gentle lapping of waves upon the shore
No longer be enough.
Let the pitchings and turnings
Of our Vessel of Light
Be unsolicited and unformed in the mind.
Let all movements simply flow
From what is happening.

Would you have a recipe here?
I think not.

Nor are you to penetrate now. Simply allow the energy to build. Do not stimulate by conscious purpose, remembering what you have read in some ego manual. Old learning is left behind here, so that the new can come in.

The fresh, the original is
Yearning to be expressed through you.
Let it come.
Move slowly with your hands,
Grasp buttocks firmly
As the tossings and turnings come stronger . . .
        Let it come!
        Let it come!
            I am within you!
            Let me come!

But let this be only preliminary. Let the Great Waves wash you ashore, still hungry, but in awe, my children, in awe of the force you have felt unleashed within you. Did you not know it was there? Perhaps you did. Perhaps not. Is it not new each time? Is not the experience recreated each time in beauty, in wonderment and surprise at all that lies within you, waiting for expression?

Transcend now all that this book would tell you, for we move into areas of "not-knowing" now, and by that, I mean not knowing with the intellect, but moving into the area of pure Feeling as our only Guide. I reside within you and I would let you know that it is here that you may walk and talk with me, in your deepest mind.

In the Silence you will find me.
Therefore, come . . .
Walk and talk with me for a moment,
That we may chart the next steps in
Our Voyage of Love together.

I am the Captain and you are the Crew
On this, our ship,
And you are being given orders as it were,
By a loving Father-figure Who
Has only your best interests as His own.

I am God, my children, manifest in a form you can understand and accept. Could you not love me more were I to come in a loving Father-form? And so I do. I use whatever loving means is available to bring you ever closer to me and to the healing which will bring you home at last, Home to your real Father and to the Love which He wishes to share with you.

But enough of heavenly themes. We are here . . . in this illusory state, believing that we are actually in bodies, and so we use these bodies, these learning devices, in order to learn that there are no limitations for us that are real. We *are* unlimited. We *are* free, all of us. I group myself with you. There is no difference between you and me, except that I have found my Unlimitedness and am always within it, and you are not . . . yet. And would you like to change that?

Then take my hand and come,
For we are going to walk
And talk on deck for a little while,
Under a placid, starry sky,
While the waves gently swoon
Under the bow of the boat. Here . . .
We shall sit for a while on this bench and talk . . .

This is, after all, a "how-to" book . . . practical, explicit and loving. It tells you what you really are and asks you to follow its plan for uncovering that Reality. It tells you that there is nothing to fear, and guides you very gently at each step into a greater flowering, a wider dimension of shared beauty.

The rose at the mother's breast
Is not purer than this book,
Even as her little child pulls at its petals.

There is beauty and power in this book, and Love, and let no man gainsay that its Author is not expert at teaching it all. I AM God. Be at peace. Let no ego fears come to tear you away in guilt and doubting.

Many are there who will renounce this book. They but turn away from their own glory and their own radiance and their own joy. Be you not among them, my child. Shy not away from all the Gifts that I have to give you here.

As we turn from the hard bench on the deck of my ship to the soft coverlets of the bed, know this: underlinings of fear may try to pinion you here. Look at them, isolate them in your mind, and let them go, asking my help in disappearing them from your experience. As you watch them evaporate into the nothingness from which they came, know this:

My love surrounds you and protects you.
You are in complete safety now.
Relax your bodies and be at peace.
There is no schedule to our being together.
There is no goal but one,
And that is to transcend the separateness of bodies
So that we may come to true Joining.
Be us about it now.

Finally! Finally! The moment has come, and the words spill out through a mind that has not so far longed enough for this to happen. Now, my scribe, now . . . hold my hand, for we reveal things not heretofore known to you, and therefore I ask you to perfect your willingness and your readiness to be with me in new ways. Long are the days when we are not manifesting together, you and I. Let this not be such a day. Come to me in perfect trust that all that comes to your mind is of me and from me. Relax into me now . . .

The crucifixion of my body was an event unparalleled in time, though many had endured the experience before me and after. It meant that I was sacrosanct as a Special Being, torn apart from my Brothers, not by the cruel tortures of the cross, but by the interpretations of those who came afterwards and lauded me into separateness from you all. I am not separate and I am here.

Tremendous atrocities have been committed in my name. Pilloryings and fires and attacks of great bestiality have been done in the name of him who came to teach only Love, for he knew that was what he was and is and forever will be, and you with him.

Pain is not real. This I learned. I felt no pain on the cross. I did not come to save a sinful world. I came to teach you what you really are. Now I come to teach you what you are in a new way.

Lie down together side by side. The Light still glows between you and around. Your toes touch, your thighs, your hands rest lightly and limply on each other's bodies. Now, take the other's face between your hands, still lying down, and ask yourselves of each other . . .

Do I really want to know the meaning of Love?
Why am I here?
Do I want to continue to be limited to this body,
Or do I want to soar,
Together with you,
Beyond this pale of littleness?

Do I really want to love you,
And therefore, myself?

Answer not lightly, my children, for the words must sink in deeply into the regions of delight . . . not those areas of surface satisfaction and pleasure, but deep within, into the delight of the soul, the rapture of spiritual union. It is here, here that you must go to find me, and it is here that you must go to find each other. You will not do this on the body level. It is impossible. Bodies cannot join. Spiritual levels are not new to you. You will recognize them as familiar when you come in truth, in faith. There is nothing to fear. All will be gently and lovingly revealed, and the wonder and amazement you will experience will be expressed as pure joy.

There. Lay all hesitation aside now, and listen. Listen to my Voice slowly, faintly rising within your mind. See? It does not sound different than your own. It is your Voice that speaks, the Voice for God, given to you by your Father in your creation. It belongs to you. It is not separate from you. It is only that you do not listen to it very often, but rather do you tune to the voice of ego, of the separated self, within you. Turn the tuning device in your mind to me now . . . see the hard plastic knob, and turn its indicator to G-O-D. There are only two stations, my children. Choose for me. And listen . . .

Tease each other a little now . . . now that you have your answers to my questions. Let the fingers trail over the body, stopping only fleetingly at the points of most sensitivity. Have you kissed as yet? Move slowly toward each other's lips, mouths slightly open, the breath of life sweetly issuing forth to mingle and bless. Press voluptuously and tease within with the tongue, rubbing ever so lightly. Let your sighs and murmurs be audible . . . let the Beloved know of your delight. Press ever more closely together . . . let the bodies mingle their contours and invite the soft flesh ever closer. Let the organs of sex be mingled as well. Let one lift one limb to permit closer affinity.

> *Snuggle together.*
> *Be as the kitten who yearns to be petted,*
> *And be the one, as well, who strokes*
> *With full, soft touches the luxuriant flesh.*
> *Explore now,*
> *Everywhere.*
> *Slowly . . . slowly . . . build to a crescendo!*

Turn swiftly now and let your lips seek another area . . . let surprises reign now as inspirations come to tell you that your creative force is flowing with you and that you are attuned to each other and to me. Let my Voice whisper in your ear all that the loving past in us would reveal.

Jesus, sweet Jesus,
Why has it never been like this before?
Why, oh why?
I thought I knew it all,
But THIS . . . THIS . . . !

Let the Silence be filled with the sound of your appreciation. Honor each other as a part, a living part of you. Say, "Thank you!," fervently, reverently, as gratitude flows within you for the experience you have consented to share.

There are not two in your bed.
There are three.
Never forget My Presence for a moment.

Let the lips of the vagina be revealed now . . . not with the fingers but in a different way. Let the woman go down on her knees, and arch her back inward, supporting her upper body weight on her hands, the knees as far apart as is comfortable.

Once again, do you trust Me?

Then let the man lie beside her, helping her with the lifting and pressing of his hand. Let her go forward and then down and back in her movements, thus revealing the vaginal opening and preparing it for the final thrusting phase. Even at this point the walls relax, and pleasures of stimulation are hers, for the sexual energies can play at being, and give her great waves of sensation.

The man watches, enjoying the beauty of the movements and the sounds of awe and pleasure that come. She turns to him, finally . . . eyes shining, full of loving awareness of his needs, and she gently pushes him on his back and reaches her lips down to his organ, and allows God to show her the way to bring him to ecstasy. He is reverent in his gratitude and fevered in his delight and bursting to completion . . . almost. More is yet to come. Not yet . . . not yet!

Roll him over now, my child, and sit astride him, letting your own organs be gently brushed as you rise on your knees and rub him with your genitals. The wetness will lubricate and you will gently trail your hands through his hair as you lean forward on each movement and touch his head, his neck, play with his ear lobes. Let your arms and hands trail behind you now onto his legs, and up to his inner thighs, gently massaging as closely as you can to the organs of delight. Are you ready then to face each other again?

Sit up in bed . . . turn to each other, and once again with a laugh of discovery, turn to the warmth and beauty of each other's bodies. Would he not drink of your splendor, my sweet, and would you not nourish him? Then let it be so. Let him lie with his head on your lap and suck the sweetness of the Spirit through your nipples.

Is it so different than before? Oh, yes! for you have let in other levels of transparent energy which transform the entire experience.

His tongue describes circles around the areolar area and pushes the nipples in. He holds the roundness of your breast within his hand with great loving care and gently squeezes and pulls a little . . . ever so little . . . to simulate a milking motion.

You know what to do now.
You need not words on a page to tell you.
You are begun in the swelling
Of the Great Wave of Light.
Let it come slowly on,
Building . . .
Building . . .
Far out in the sea of your passion.

But do not control it.
Do not push it . . .
Do not pull it . . .
Let it build of its own accord.
It will take care of itself.
I will take care of you.

Allow Me in now, my sweet, into your vagina. Lie down on your back and open wide your legs. I will give you impulses of the greatest ecstasy . . . second only to his, my love, second only to his. Remember only that I come in God-Love, not in sensual passion, and I come to show you what is really yours, to teach you the capacity of your own being to produce and share ecstasy. The swelling pulsations that seek out the depths of your vagina are from me. I am there. But not as man-form. As God-Love. There is a difference. See me not as man. That is not why I am here. The form you seek you will not find. Only know that I am here. I am here to teach you. For in fact it is you who create these feelings by your permission-giving. I but teach you what you really are . . . a radiant and beautiful Being of Light, so beautiful that you see yourself as Giver of Light now, and Love.

Slowly the radiance forms between your legs and

within your lower abdomen . . . lovingly, gently, the God-energy massages and titillates. The waves of ecstasy are not unlike sexual union. But they are finer, more ethereal, but preparations for what is to come.

> *I AM to come.*
> *I AM to come within you.*
> *The God-Self which I AM is within you,*
> *And I AM to come . . .*
> *In your union am I reborn.*
> *Each time you come together in love*
> *Am I reborn into your relationship,*
> *And slowly, ever so slowly,*
> *You will come to fruition,*
> *To completion in Me.*

You are more than what you see. You are more than what you know. Be about discovering that now, as you turn, my little one, to give your partner his turn. Let me help you now, telling you what he would like, moving your hands, your body, your limbs, into positions that will fill him with delight. Try placing your vagina against his open mouth. Be not affrighted if this is new to you. He will respond with great sensitivity. But linger not long in any one place . . .

Let the crescendo that is beating within you
Keep you not passive longer!
NOW! WHIRL!
Whirl with the cosmic dance that is beating
Its rhythm within your beings.
Do not let the music stop
By hesitating for one second!
Leap into the revolving whirl
With the unpremeditated movement
That unleashes your Divinity.
NOW! my child, NOW!

Light a candle now,
Both together.
Let the music of the soul swell
Into a finer, more fragrant tune.
Let the energies abate somewhat,
For we have an eternity, do we not, tonight?

Timelessness is upon us.
Love is upon us.
My Voice is upon you, and My Touch . . .

I send a pulsation of energy to you, my son, radiant energy that enlivens and glows within your groin. You turn, not in desperate outpouring of force destined only for release, but with ever greater intensity to tell her of what you are feeling. Talk to her . . . tell her of her beauty and the meaning of the Light that you see shining out from her. Tell her that she is more than body to you. She is the essence of God and she is becoming visible to you as that essence.

Let the unfolding of your Love be true and visible to her, that you care for her for what she truly is, and not the gratification her body can give to yours. You must go beyond this so that she feels valued in the essence of what she is, and in the essence of what you are, will you recognize what you have given yourself . . . the gift of the Universe, the gift of Self-realization. You come closer . . . ever closer.

Now . . . respite . . . ever so briefly, for we cannot go on without a prayer here. Will you join me?

Father,
Please be with us now
As we go on to completion
Of this Act of Love.

We would have this be
A Gift for You,
Showing You that by seeing Your Son
In all His spiritual splendor,
And loving only that,
We reach to Your altar
With this pure and untrammeled sacrament.

Pour upon us please,
The sacred oil of Your blessings,
Upon this union and each other.

Thank You, Father.

We begin the ending now. Know it to be so. Know it to be the Will of God that you do this. Let there be peace about it, and Perfection. Perfection is of the Spirit, not of the body. Hold only to that. What comes will be perfect. It cannot be otherwise. Let no disappointment nor judgment stand in your way of realizing all that God would have you learn here. He is with you. Be content.

You have a favorite position? If so, assume it. If not, let me suggest mine. Hold her aloft, my son, ever so lightly for a moment, if this is possible, and then let her sink slowly down beside you . . . on your preferred side. Now let your eyes, your lips, your arms, your torsos, your genitals all merge. Let there not be two now, not on any level. Put aside all feelings of hurry and forcing. Only choose to *let* things happen.

Her breasts press upon you . . . your penis penetrates into the folds of her vagina, making brief insertions, little journeys to try out the waters. Let it be comfortable and warm and wet before you go on further. Move the tip of the penis so slowly, so gently, upon the lubricated clitoris, around and up and down, and then ever so quickly, a surreptitious and surprise entrance but partway into the Place of Wonder.

Atrophy of desire is impossible now. The untrammeled wetness cries for entrance and the willingness is NOW! Not with force, but ever so slowly, so that she cries out with delight. Yes, my son, NOW! As far as you can, but not to completion, not to the filling . . . until you assume the final posture . . . your own, and let the movements dictate their own accord.

You will be moved. You will know.
The depths are not to be resisted.
The gentle clasping which meets them
And holds you there,
Sucking,
Caressing,
She will know how to do.

She gently milks you into ecstasy, my son,
And so you see,
Beyond the tumultuous pleasures of the orgasm,
Her own lips cry out
As bereavement is replaced by a vision of Light
That embraces and warms and endears your
Oneness . . .
Your baptism,
The true Baptism into God.

Here you cannot describe . . .
Now you do not know one another as bodies,
But you have experienced a Joining
That is simply a reaching to your own true level
of Being.

Here am I with you,
Joining in that ecstasy.
Here am I with you,
Smiling in blessing
As you free yourselves from the dark shadows
Of your past on earth.
Still are you there,
But all is transformed,
And you come to know what you are and what
she is.

And you will greet each other when you awaken with these words, joyfully spoken:

Father, thank you! for helping me to find in this Other my true Self! No longer shall I fear you nor believe you wish me harm. No longer are you a stern taskmaster to me, watching over my fate with dogged persistence in giving me suffering.

I know you now as a Father of Love. Nevermore will my lips be stayed in praising you for your Gifts, Father, for I see that in giving is my receiving, and in our giving of ourselves to You in this union, have we come to receive the greatest Gift of all . . . the knowledge of Ourselves in You.

The cry of joy may take many forms. It does not matter. You will not remember these words, most likely. Only remember the prayer that longs to issue from your lips in holy gratitude and Love, the prayer of thanksgiving that God has not left any loving means outside of His caring and concern for you.

My children, there is more. Come. Take my hand. Gently look into each other's eyes and tell me what you see . . . Let the Silence enfold you. The words that later come are heart words, and you will know them as they issue forth. Let them come . . .

Turn away now but to cleanse, and help each other . . . with warm cloths, with towels, with a resplendent bath. Let you lave one another with the energy-water and be ever more close, not letting the experience end with the abysmal explosion. For from your depths did it not come? From depths you did not know you had?

From the abyss of the Father's Love it came, my children, and its sparkling beauty and tremendous power did not override you, nor shut from your awareness the Presence of each other as Sons of God. Do not lose it now. Carry it with you as you go about your next activities, whatever they may be. If you go to sleep, do it lovingly, in each other's arms . . . communicating whether by silence or by words, the rapturous trailings of your Experience together.

The stardust lies glittering
Upon our footsteps
As we walk down the Path together,
Dreaming once again of Home,
And lighting the way
For all to follow after.

Come! We have far to go!
A world awaits your saving Grace.
Share your Experience.
Do not let your Light be hidden,
But let others know of what is possible.

In the sharing is the healing.
In the sharing is the teaching.
In the sharing is the Son of God made whole.

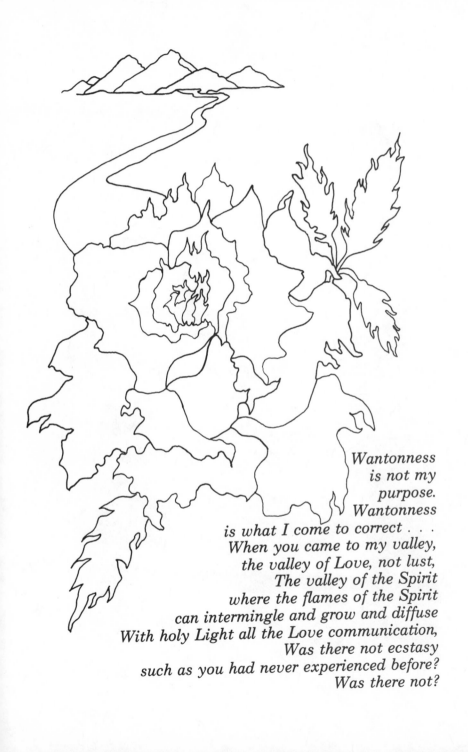

Wantonness
is not my
purpose.
Wantonness
is what I come to correct . . .
When you came to my valley,
the valley of Love, not lust,
The valley of the Spirit
where the flames of the Spirit
can intermingle and grow and diffuse
With holy Light all the Love communication,
Was there not ecstasy
such as you had never experienced before?
Was there not?

Epilogue

There is a book which we shall tell you about now. It has been mentioned before. Its name is Come No More To Altars Of Nothingness. It is a book by Jesus the Christ, recorded by this scribe, and brought to you here in the form of excerpts which have to do with the subject of the sexual relationship.

You must come to understand eventually, my children, that the words you hear through this scribe are my own. I have chosen every word in this book, and in Come No More To Altars Of Nothingness. I have many different ways of communicating through my scribes, with my scribes and with you. But never let it be said that any mind chose the words in these books but mine.

Now we will share tidbits with you . . . carefully designed and chosen to entice you into the entire manuscript when it is completed and in book form. I am unabashed in doing this, for hardly could a greater help be given to you on your Path Home.

If the wording seems puzzling and unromantic, know it was carefully chosen to be that way. I do not make mistakes, my children. If you see mistakes, know that is your choice. Even as I teach this scribe, so do I teach you.

The natural mystification that will come over your minds in the reading of this material is deliberately created. It will edge you on ever closer to your God, help you ever to desire more of me and my Teachings in all their many forms.

Wander now, with me, through these pages. Get a feel for my flavor, for my personality, for I do have such a blending and it is expressed here. I am individual, even as you. I am also One, even as you. It is a paradox to be resolved in loving delight someday, unless you have already had the Experience.

Come No More to Altars of Nothingness is not like any book ever written before in the history of mankind. You will remember these words often as you make this journey through the material. It is not going to fit your expectations, for there is no way for you to have expectations for something so unusual, so beyond the ken of those whose minds have been conditioned and trained into set patterns.

We break all the molds in this book, all the mind-sets of the ego centuries in this ego world, for we go to present a new picture of the Son of God as manifested in my life and in my presence down through the centuries, a presence felt rather than seen, heard rather than listened to, for, my children, who has really listened since that time when I came to earth so long ago? How could a book written by Jesus the Christ have been created and accepted until now, when a New Age is about to dawn upon this riddled and torn and agonizing earth?

This scribe receives my words right now at great speed as she types, with no mentation going on in her mind, other than to hear my words. This is a co-created book, and yet one in which every word was chosen by me. This scribe participated not in that choice, but did participate in its writing by a process which we will explain as we go. Be content now with this admonition:

A closed mind will never be able to grasp this material in its entirety. A judgmental mind will never be able to learn the God lessons of Come No More . . .

Come to me now, each of you, as we begin this momentous journey together, for so it will be, a walk with Jesus the Christ, as he speaks through this scribe and others. We shall make it alive for you as we go, and its aliveness will give you irrefutable Truth.

Reach beyond the words now, my children, for these times bespeak of much that is unusual to your present perception, perhaps. Perhaps not. I will not judge. Be ye ready to come without judgment.

But what if it's really him?

Let that be the answer to any ego doubts that may rise in your holy minds . . . aye, what if it is *really* Jesus the Christ who speaks to you? *What if it is?*

It is, my children, it is! Be of good cheer, and know that I *am* with you. You will come to know me as a person as we go through these pages together, and the resulting relationship that will be formed will give you much joy and peace . . . a ready help in all life situations. Is that so terrible? *(laughing)*

Yes, I laugh . . . and sometimes, I weep . . . and sometimes I am jocular . . . and sometimes my voice bespeaks sternness and admonishments . . . in fact, my personality as man will come to be revealed to you even as it was revealed so many years ago in another time and another place. Some of you were there, even then, and that, too, shall be revealed as we go.

Perfect Trust, the development of perfect faith in God and in His Plan for your lives . . . it is this to which we go, for it is in this that your perfect happiness and your perfect security and peace also lie. Come with me now . . . hear how all of this happened . . . and *judge not . . . judge not . . .*

Let these words ring in your ears whenever you hear a voice of doubt and fear begin to creep in. There is no cause for fear, for this is a Voice only of Love, the Love of the Father, the Love of the Son, the Love of the Holy Spirit. These are my words. I am Jesus the Christ. Need you know more?

Excerpt from:

COME NO MORE TO ALTARS OF NOTHINGNESS
Oct. 28, 1980

This is a page written expressly for inclusion into the book called, **A Spiritual Sex Manual.** It will also appear in **Come No More** . .'s printing. It is an appeal, my children, for your help.

I cannot come through each of you as yet in visible form as I can with this scribe and others. But it is my wish to do so. If you will but give permission to hear the Voice for God, this experience can be yours as well. Not all are ready to hear my Voice. Not all are ready to come to their Agreements with me. But know this and know it well . . .

The ending of the world as you know it can be close. It is imperative that all come to spirit in the way that is best for them, and give renewed interest and yearning to the cause for world peace. Many come in my name and do not see their mistakes, but the time for clarification is now, and the tools for clarification are set before you:

> *If what you hear is not loving,*
>   *it is not of me.*
> *If what you do is not loving,*
>   *it is not of me.*
> *If what you think is not loving,*
>   *it is not of me.*
> *How much more simple can it be?*

Excerpt from:

COME NO MORE TO ALTARS OF NOTHINGNESS
Nov. 25, 1979

"Imperative is the time, my sweet, for I would have you know that Jesus the Christ has descended into your midst once again to orchestrate the day's happenings . . . be you ready?"

"Yes."

"Finally it has begun, my love. The Great Reclamation Project by God which shall enhance the projections of the ego and turn them to spirit. We shall reach the emancipation of the spirit through the body and do it with flair and style. It may seem like body identification at first, but soon the true meaning and Purpose will be revealed, and the ego's own game shall be overturned. We go to Heaven in every loving way there is, and we go in style and pleasure, for yes, is it not pleasurable to give Love through the body, is it not pleasurable to communicate Love through the very sensations and feelings that the ego turns to degradation and lust and loathing?

"The sexual impulses are holy as they are first materialized from the Unborn, and fashioned into form and sensation within the body. And then the ego takes them, colors them with 'dirt' and transforms them into revilement and paper lust acts in magazines and books, lewd and erotic degradations captured on film and displayed before eyes and minds aching with hunger for Love. A rotten feast for the rottenness of the ego spawn lying as embryonic seeds in the mind!

COME NO MORE TO ALTARS OF NOTHINGNESS
Nov. 25, 1979 (continued)

"Why, my children, why? Is not the sexual act capable of being pure and loving and kindly as well, and is the miracle impulse of Love not able to be expressed through the body, and transmuted into the spiritual fire of joining, spiritual Joining? The embarrassment people have over the body and its sexual use only gives rise to the pornography that hides and feeds in dark corners. Uncover it all, and let it be exposed to the fresh air of Love and sunshine!

"Wantonness is not my purpose. Wantonness is what I come to correct. There could be no wantonness if the true purpose of sex became the spiritual Joining with one another and God, and it is so easy to release, so easy to relax into the joy of this mode of being, is it not, my child? Have not you and your husband experienced this in a sudden and swift descent from the ego mountaintops of withdrawal and isolation? When you came to my valley, the valley of Love, not lust, the valley of the Spirit where the flames of the spirit can intermingle and grow and diffuse with holy Light all the Love communication, was there not ecstasy such as you had never experienced before? Was there not?"

"It was amazing. Yes."

"Need I convince you, my love?" *(quietly)* - - -

"I am convinced."

"Lust and Love are often mistaken, my children, so intertwined as to make it impossible to pull them apart and examine them for what they are. True spiritual Joining is possible, and it is mete and right for it to be accomplished through

COME NO MORE TO ALTARS OF NOTHINGNESS
Nov. 25, 1979 (continued)

the act of sex. Sex is procreation, but it is also our first
priority in the manifestation of Love between persons of the
same or opposite sex. The drive of the body has as its center
the hunger of the spirit to join, to be unseparate in the illusion, to find the true Identity that lingers forever untouched
and unfulfilled in the center of each being. The usual approach to sexual fulfillment does nothing to satisfy the real
need.

"Be you ready to hear how my scribe and her husband in-
vited me into their bed and into their sexual expression last
night as a supreme example of trust in the unusual ramifica-
tions of their special Function in me?

"Knowing that this material was to be shared has set up a
slight residual tension in my usually open and relaxed scribe,
my reader. This is not an easy place for her to be. Know that
and be patient with the words as they come, my child. You
are doing well this morning, but sharing your marital bed
with the world is another giant step, is it not? And especially
in the way that it happened?"

"Yes."

"Are you unhappy with me and my participation in your
love-making last night?"

"Oh, no! It was wonderful!"

"Then relax and share so that we may help thousands of
others to new heights of spiritual unfoldment. For you see,
my readers, the act of sex is as valid a way to get to God as

COME NO MORE TO ALTARS OF NOTHINGNESS
Nov. 25, 1979 (continued)

any other, if it is done as an act of true Love, if the Oneness
is recognized above and beyond all else. I bring my scribe
and her husband to the full appreciation and experiencing of
this Oneness with each step we take together. I asked them to
give me permission to be with them in their bed last night
and to direct their actions, step by step, by speaking through
one to the other, alternating this experience. The joy and
fulfillment and ecstasy of their experience was a delight to
them both, and gave them a dimension of sexuality never
before experienced by either. The chagrin of my scribe to
have my 'holy' image tarnished in the eyes of the world with
this material is amusing to me, but I feel ever so tenderly
toward her for her concern. We break down the old idols,
remember? *Be you about it with me!*

"Now. Let us resume. Alternative plans have been made by
God for the joining of souls in the illusion. You may come to
Him in many ways, my children, and there is a perfect Path
for each of you. For each Son there is a perfect Way. For
some it is the act of sex. Tantric Buddhism has long held this
as a valid approach to God. Recognize only that lip service to
whatever way is chosen is *not* a way to Him.

"Therefore, I admonish you with great alacrity to listen to
my words and give credence to them as a possibility in your
lives. God would not have you in lack in any way, and to
allow ego distortions between you in the functioning together
of your bodies in sexual loveplay is to be out of alignment
with God's Plan for your lives. Such sexual role-play is effec-
tive only in those whose ego needs have been, at least tem-
porarily, quelled, so that the Oneness of spirit can be

Come No More To Altars Of Nothingness
Nov. 25, 1979 (continued)

manifest. Steps are needed. Practice is needed. We but unfold for you now the first step . . .

"Place yourselves, my children, in my hands in perfect trust. Invite me into your bed with you, welcome me with a formal statement so that I may come without disturbing or invading your privacy. There is no time when I come to you in error, any of you, and those who are ready to undertake this unusual journey with me will be richly rewarded in spirit.

"Place yourselves totally in my hands now, my children, and allow me to direct each motion of your bodies, or non-motion. I will call for stillness; I will call for activity; I will be specific as to each movement and time it all perfectly for you. Insanity? No, I but teach you in this as in all things, to clear away forever the ego confusion which holds you in such pain in your sexual relationships. Between man and woman, between woman and man . . . God makes no distinctions. Between man and man, woman and woman . . . God makes no distinctions. Be with me now in perfect trust as we journey to the melding of spirit.

"Foresee no distinctions between you. Allow your bodies to melt into One Experience. Let the joy of union become a foreseeable event in your minds, even before the physical steps are taken. Release yourselves from all effects of grievances before beginning by turning all grievances over to the Holy Spirit for vanishing. Let all be still before God's Holy Light and watch the play unfold in perfect trust.

"Embrace each other lovingly and fully before the play begins. Feel the warmth and comfort of the body as an ex-

Come No More To Altars Of Nothingness
Nov. 25, 1979 (continued)

pression of the Love that waits within. See the Love that is expressed through the body as the intimacy for which you long. Center not on the physical sensation, but on the joining of souls. Remind yourself of your Oneness at every step of the way, and let the sense of separate bodies blend into that Oneness. See the Great Rays of Light merge into One, overlaid with trust and ecstasy as the Joining is completed. Step by step I will take you, even as I took them last night. The peaks of ecstasy which they both experienced yet ring in them as perfect and complete fulfillment. The Oneness Experience with the Universe did not come last night, but it will. They but go step by step.

"Their marriage has long been beset with difficulties in the sexual area, poor communication, ego grievances, mismatching by God in may ways, the 'typical' marriage with needs being met in some areas and not in others. The special relationship in its fullest, most negative mode became theirs at times, but at others, there was a comfort and friendship which has persisted as a single thread through their many years together.

"They come to me now as partners in a play without an end, though they know it not. They will be together many times again, working with me, playing with me, following my directives in the illusion. They are my trusted helpers and friends, and they but complete their parts perfectly. They are not special, any more than you, my readers. You can do what they do. They have no 'special gifts;' they are not 'highly evolved' souls to be set on a pedestal above the rest. They are 'ordinary people' even as you, come to do great things by accepting what they really are . . . holy Sons of

Come No More To Altars Of Nothingness
Nov. 25, 1979 (continued)

God Himself, which is what you are, though you may deny it with blind vehemence.

"It is time for this chapter to close now, and your questions will be many. Come to me with them, and know that they will be answered. We will write of this subject in another book in due time, which will lay out in perfect detail the specific steps. My scribe is not ready. My scribe trembleth! Why, my child, why? Let it go, my little one! You were splendid!"

This is new material, my Mary, to be scribed by you this day. I follow not the usual format in the writing of this book, but give you pieces to put together to allow you this creative experience in its writing, even while I choose the words. Now hear this: our subject for today is maximal interpretation of the end result of the book called, A Spiritual Sex Manual.

Mary, clear your mind now of all doubt and listen. Simply type the words you hear without concern for their meaning. Do not place this unnecessary burden on yourself today. Much will come that will be startling. You need not be concerned. Do not project its effect upon the world . . . nor upon yourself. Just write the words. Then go back with me later and we will take a look together at the words of Jesus the Christ through you. Remember to suspend all judgment now as we go . . .

Follow me, my children, now as we go to the end of our book. Much will follow that will perhaps disturb you. Much may come through this scribe now that may give you great discomfort, but know this:

*The Truth is true,
And nothing else is true.*

This means that all illusion is false, and you have no recourse but to come to this realization some day.

I do not come to shock you nor to blame anyone. I do not come to pronounce judgment of any kind. I do come to tell you of another way to live in this world that will bring you peace and happiness . . . those seeming "will-o-the-wisps" mankind has followed through the centuries, constantly being pursued and never being found, at least by the mainstream of mankind.

Nevertheless, it *is* possible, and I bring you but one way in this book to reach that peace. I cannot come to you here with all of the answers and all of the ways in which God may be found within you. I cannot tell you how to do more than give your willingness for all that you are within to come into view in your life. It must be done step by step, and sometimes the way is painful because you have falsely believed that pain is the way to growth and learning. It is only so because of your belief . . . not for any other reason.

What you really are conflicts with what you think you are. Truth cannot change. Nor can I. I am Jesus the Christ speaking through this scribe with words that are not her choosing. She is Mary . . . I am Jesus . . . in this our ritual prepared but for the choosing which you are now being asked to do.

I have slept with this scribe . . . in this lifetime. In this body has she known me sexually. You may be aghast at this, and yet I tell you that it is so.

It is necessary to present to the world an accounting of this to negate forever the futileness that besets you all when you come to the sexual act. I cannot come to each of you in this same way, nor will I. Do not long for a love affair with Jesus the Christ. This scribe consented to this because it was her Function. I come to no other in this way. This does not make her special. It means that she had come to a point in her spiritual development that made her immune to ego attachment regarding this matter. Now I come to her to tell her that the ending of this book means the ending of that manifestation of our relationship. From now on her sexual relationship with her husband will be only as described in this book . . . even as I have shared it with you. There will be no personhood of Jesus the Christ seeming to fill her body with the illusion of man.

Know, my Mary, that tremendous changes are in store for you. You must give up the prayer of your heart that asks for the cloistered life. That part is over now for you. Send away the love of privacy and seclusion and peaceful solitude, for that must now be obtained only in the press of ongoing events and activities. It will be more important than ever that you practice your one-pointed concentration upon me, and allow me to deal with the exigencies of your life. You have been well trained for this. Long not for the old days of peaceful seclusion in the wilderness. I have you now, and much will happen soon . . . you must make your peace in the midst of the most challenging of situations. Learn well, my child, learn well, for the world will not leave you alone, once this book goes out. Come. Now.

And so she came, knowingly, trusting in this role she was to play, feeling the inner rightness of her devotion, turning all else aside to follow her heart's commitment . . . without question.

Circumscribe all cries of witchcraft and devil-worship, my children, as you read this material. Know that I am Jesus, and that in my opportunity to be with this woman, I did simulate in her mind an actual physical relationship with me. Or was it real? What is "real?" What is "simulation?" Can you tell me? Or shall I tell you that in this relationship was Jesus the Christ made manifest again as man? For I was, my children, I was. Read on.

Excerpt from:

COME NO MORE TO ALTARS OF NOTHINGNESS
Nov. 30, 1979

"Stay with me a moment, Mary, while we tell of our evening together last night, and of our reunion in the bed of our choice, bridging the centuries with our loving commitment to be together in this time . . .

"The heat of passion grows dear with the remembering, and the time of sweetness is brought to life again. The passage of time meant nothing as we relived again the sweetness of the memories. I catapulted you back through the centuries to the appearance, the settings, the tastes and smells of biblical times. The aroma of love reappeared between us as I channeled myself through the body of your husband into your arms once again. The Father's Wish was fulfilled last night, and the time will be repeated tonight, as the nuptial celebrations continue. The notice was short and the time astagger during yesterday's abrupt introduction of the new event. Now is the time to share the feelings you experienced, my Mary, as the marriage consummation was enacted."

"Jesus, it isn't easy . . . "

"Tell of the changes in your husband, my love."

"There were alterations in my husband's voice and demeanor and actions, and sounds of passion so distinctly different that I believed his body was being shared with Jesus. His voice, usually mild-mannered and soft and of medium tonal range, became a deep baritone, and passionate sounds such as I have never heard before came from his lips. He was continually reminding me to listen and watch innerly for

COME NO MORE TO ALTARS OF NOTHINGNESS
Nov. 30, 1979 (continued)

scenes from the past. As thoughts of desired physical stimulation came into my mind, they were answered through his body actions, which had never happened before. The mind in my husband's body knew my every unspoken thought and responded to it.

"Afterwards my husband told me he felt he actually left the scene at times, and it was hard for him to maintain his focus, both physical and mental, for he was so absent, and Jesus had to call him back to maintain his attention.

"At the peak of passion, hearing the words coming through him as the words of Jesus, I found myself crying out, 'Jesus, Jesus . . . it's really you!' And I knew that it was. Lying in my arms was the man I had loved so well almost two thousand years ago. I was shown the appearance of my body then as well as his. I found myself watching scenes from long ago, reviving actions and rituals from the past . . . things being given to my mind. At one moment, I felt a quick fear when I first realized and heard the different sounds, the voice changes that were so dramatic and different. Then I heard Jesus' voice in my mind, reassuring me, and I let that go, and flowed with the flow."

"How do you feel this morning, Mary? Only a few hours of sleep have you had."

"I feel a peace and sweet contentment and deep happiness. I do not understand the reasons for the experience last night. Upon asking this morning I was told that Love was enough reason . . . there did not have to be a greater God-Purpose

COME NO MORE TO ALTARS OF NOTHINGNESS
Nov. 30, 1979 (continued)

than that. It was simply the time of fulfillment of the ancient
pledge Mary and Jesus had made to each other."

"Do you believe it was me, my Mary?"

"Yes, I know that it was."

"We go Home soon."

"Yes."

"The bridge grows shorter in your mind when I stand on
the other side."

"There is no bridge, Jesus. Please wake me up."

"When the time is right, my sweet."

"I place it in your hands then."

"Go to your day now, my child. We carry with us the
memories of our reunion, the power and magnificence of our
joining, the sweet surrender. The cries of the joining rend
through the overlays of the centuries, making all things whole
between us now. Surrender your day to me, my Mary, even
as I have taught you. Come to me, my Mary. Now."

Lightness is come upon the face of the deep, and lying here, side by side, they came to know Each Other as themselves, and the ending of the dream of separateness is over forever. Now . . . now, my children, hear this:

The essence of your Togetherness
Is now within your grasp.
This book walks with you,
And you are not alone,
But ever and anon my Voice will come,
Trailing the stardust as a path to Home.
See it not in a far distant sky,
But within you . . . yes! within!

Traveling far across the globe will not bring you closer to holiness. Reading and reaching for dusty tomes of ancient wisdom will not bring you peace. It must be chosen. There is no other way. Simple is Salvation, and yet you who would set it in complexity must have your way as well.

This book is not that way. It was not so intended. It is a simple book, telling of a not-so-simple Love Experience. Was I ever one to need flowery words and inescapable platitudes? That is not the Jesus you remember who fed the multitudes and multiplied the loaves and fishes. I need no rhetoric. Nor do you. You need the simple Truth, unvarnished and unveiled, and I come to give it to you.

I am come again. No words can bring me closer to you, for I am already there . . . within. But you need help in remembering, in realizing that the subterfuges which your mistakes would create in your minds are not real, and need not be accepted.

Accept me, instead. Accept me into your hearts and into your beds and into your relationships, for I am the Father and the Son and the Holy Spirit, all One, indivisible, as are you.

Relent now in your choices. Let the Love of God melt the hard resistance into the easy flow of Love. You know what I mean . . . not with the mind, but with the heart. Deep within, you know, my children, what I mean. Let that tiny impulse of Love reach out across the gap that seems to separate you from me, and let the eternity of that Instant keep you ever in God's Joy.

What has this to do with A Spiritual Sex Manual, you say? And what is the purpose of our book? Some will come to it and experience Eternity within its covers. Others will consummate the joining in a perfect and shining moment of bliss. Others will walk through, greatly enhanced, spurred on by the Voice and the Presence they find therein. We walk on, my child. This is the ending of our book. Come . . . the path grows clear just around the bend, and your Guide would lead you there. The lights of Home beckon. They grow faint when you forget your dedication to your own happiness. Surpass yourself now. Drop all else and walk on . . . unburdened and in firm resolve, for you go onward to a Love that hungers as you do.

And would you keep Him waiting?

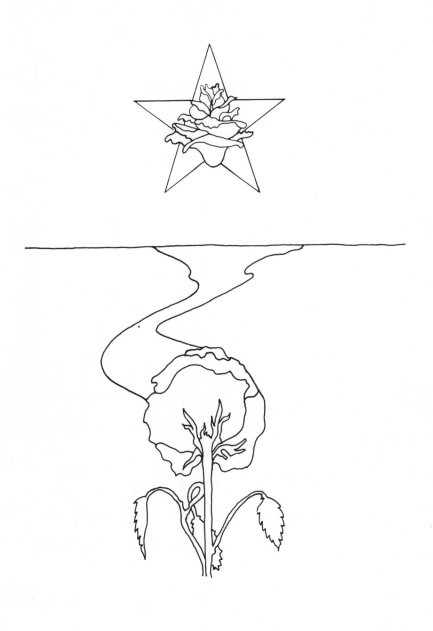

To The Scribe
January 24, 1982

The matrix of the future lies in you as a seed. Let it unfold at its own rate, gently, slowly. It is rising as a star in the night of ego, and gently assisted by the efforts of your Helpers. Let me guide the timing. Know I shall always tell you of the lessons unlearned and face, together with you, the next step.

We here thank you for your willingness to hold to the incredible, literally "not credible," vision you have been given. Hold it as an embryo deep within your mind . . . not as a burden, but a loving act of nourishment and protection. Those qualities you hold so well in your mind and heart will see you through the journey, and the end will not be as the beginning.

Refuse access to all who come not in my name, but when a name appears in your consciousness and you turn to me for approval and help, then trust that response. The power of my name is not to be doubted, and the protection it affords is absolute.

Refuse, as well, all claim to A Spiritual Sex Manual as an authoress. The copyright will be held by you . . . in trust . . . and that Agreement will be written and put into the book. As scribe you are not responsible for the writing. There will be a statement to that effect. You are responsible for the trust invested in you as scribe and deliverer of the manuscript, as testimonial to the process, as teacher of the concepts.

That will be enough to fill your life with tasks, as you well know, and so you ask, "How shall these great communities come about and what is my role in them?" And I say, as mother and nurturer, as embryo is held in the womb, so the mind-womb holds the community . . . and waits . . . for the perfect development of the fetus and its subsequent birth in perfect timing into the world.

You are my scribe. You are my teacher. You are not to foresee the entire development of these centers as your responsibility. Many will come to do the work. Relinquish the mental burden you carry with you.

You are scribe and seer; you are poet and matrix; you are teacher and lecturer; you are talisman and rose. And you are my Mary. Never forget that you are my Mary. As the seed grows in the darkness of the earth, so A Spiritual Sex Manual has grown in the fastnesses of mental space you have so willingly provided it.

The interim time before publication will see many changes, but clear let it be that you stand for me and you support my hand as Author of this work. Divine be it, and Divinity shall sign its name in it, using your hand, your fingers, your mind, your body. The energy that moves those fingers that hold the pen shall be the same energy that moves the Perfection of the planet into place.

Doubt not, little one. I take full responsibility for what I have authored, and I tell you true what it is that I shall say through you.

To All My Brothers

Sign me forever as faithful to you in thought, word and deed. Know that the copyright of this book is held in Trust by this scribe during her lifetime, and will pass to The Christ Foundation upon the termination of this lifetime on earth. So will the other books each be for you and for the world a testimonial to my presence among you, and a seed planted for future generations to come.

Scenes from the next book will be equally . . . distasteful or uplifting . . . beautiful or ugly. Which will you choose? The next book, Jesus and Mary, will astound and delight you as well. The finality of our relationship as Jesus and Mary comes with the creation of that book. I tell you now, and her, so that you will know the ending is a final farewell of a love affair that began long ago, and has continued through the centuries.

Is it true? Is it untrue? What does it matter? You know that within yourselves lie the seeds of a New Age where the subject of reincarnation will receive much clarification and extension. Be patient and wait. The new book will reveal much and the poignancy of that time and that relationship will be impressed upon your minds in ways that will be new to you and to her. Plead not for escape, my Mary, for you hold within your mind the memory of an experience that will free your Brothers from many sad misconceptions. Have the courage now to hold the matrix of the new book within your mind and heart, even as you held this one for so many years.

All proceeds from the writings will be used for the furtherance of God's Work. We invite your participation in all the ways there are. Let not this invitation be misconstrued, but know that the forms of manifestation are many, and God's Work needs them all. We mold the energy of the Universe into form and use it for the emancipation of the mind of God's Son. It is called Salvation. Are you ready to assist?

I come to find my Brothers
Who are lost on the path of darkness.
I come to find the ninety and nine as well.
I come to each of you
Through the thin veil that seems to separate us,
And hold out my hand to each one of you
As brother, as friend.

I sign my name here, as it was signed before, in trust, in Love, and in perfect confidence. Let this be for you a sign that speaks to you of my presence within *you*, and bespeaks to you of the Presence of God in your souls.

Jesus the Christ